The BocaYente's Slice of Life

Phyllis Dinerman

Copyright © 2005 by Phyllis Dinerman

All rights reserved. No part of this book shall be reproduced or transmitted in any form or by any means, electronic, mechanical, magnetic, photographic, including photocopying, recording or by any information storage and retrieval system, without prior written permission of the publisher. No patent liability is assumed with respect to the use of the information contained herein. Although every precaution has been taken in the preparation of this book, the publisher and author assume no responsibility for errors or omissions. Neither is any liability assumed for damages resulting from the use of the information contained herein.

ISBN 0-7414-2350-2

Please visit the author's website:
www.bocayente.com

Published by:

INFINITY
PUBLISHING.COM

1094 New De Haven Street, Suite 100
West Conshohocken, PA 19428-2713
Info@buybooksontheweb.com
www.buybooksontheweb.com
Toll-free (877) BUY BOOK
Local Phone (610) 941-9999
Fax (610) 941-9959

Printed in the United States of America

Printed on Recycled Paper

Published January 2005

Acknowledgments

My sincere thanks to Jerry, my beloved husband, who allowed me to put in print, for all to read, the many funny incidents of our married life. Without his encouragement and support, this *Slice of Life* would still be an idea unfulfilled.

Thanks to my son, Bradley, who designed my website; and to both my sons and their families for allowing me to share in the joys of their life.

To my grandchildren, you're the Loves of my life and you put a smile on my face.

To my Florida friends who allowed me to print about our summer vacation.

To my northern friends who never knew if and when they would read about themselves in my column.

Many thanks to my editor, Nancy Butler Ross, for her help and advice in putting forth this book.

And, to my parents, both deceased: You would have been so proud of me. I hope you're looking down and *kvelling*.

Praise for Phyllis Dinerman's
The BocaYente's Slice of Life

"Phyllis Dinerman is a modern Yiddishe mama. With an eye for irony and a humorous intelligence, she gossips, she kvells and above all, she frets over the challenges we all face in coping with everyday life in middle-class America."

----Mark R. Arnold, Editor/Publisher,
Jewish Journal/North of Boston

"This book will make you laugh and bring a slice of Florida sunshine into your life"

----Phyllis Karas, author of
The Onassis Women: An Eyewitness Account,
The Redemption of Eddie Macke,
and a columnist for the Boston Herald.

"This book is an absolute 'must read.' I was told I must read it or I was out of the will."

----Brad Dinerman, older son

"BocaYente...humorous and heartwarming...It makes us laugh...it makes us cry to think that people will actually read about us. Please be kind."

----Davida Dinerman, daughter-in-law of eldest son

"Clever, amusing, laughed out loud...and I had to write this or my mother would have 'shot me.'"

----Michael Dinerman, younger son

"I read the "BocaYente" with a smile on my face. There are side splitting laughs. She is as funny on paper as she is in the flesh."

----Sheryl Lappin Levy,
President of Jewish Federation, Women's Division

"After reading the Boca Yente's book, you'll have a lot of laughs, some of it at my expense. That's OK, since it is all done in good taste. This is one great book."

----Jerry Dinerman, *the BocaYente's husband.*
(So what else could I say?)

"Advice, Schmice ---- We all give it. Now it is our turn to get it with love and humor!"

----Helaine R. Hazlett (another Jewish mother)
Hazlett is President of Temple Beth El
in Swampscott, MA.;
mother of 4, grandmother of 9.

TABLE OF CONTENTS

The Birth of the BocaYente i

1. The Lost Tribes of Israel 1
2. Our First Apartment in Florida 4
3. I Was the Only One Wearing a One- Piece Bathing Suit 6
4. School at my Age? 8
5. "Can You Hear Me? Can You Hear Me Now?" 10
6. The Eye of the Needle 12
7. A Hot Flash is a Gender Discriminatory Action 15
8. Sshh…Don't Talk About It…… 17
9. Vanity, Thy Name is Woman 19
10. Cellulite is America's Number One Most Wanted Enemy 21
11. Welcome College Alumni 26
12. Tennis Warriors 29
13. What Your Car Says About You 31
14. Nothing Beats a Toothache!! 33
15. I Didn't Steal Your Shopping Cart 35
16. I Refuse to Travel North in the Winter 39
17. Give Me a Hardwood Floor Any Day 42
18. How to Run the Thermostat in Cold Weather in Florida 44
19. I Think the Air-conditioning is Broken… 45
20. Go West, Young Man 48
21. Does the Bus Driver Know the Way? 50
22. Snowbirds Fly South <u>after</u> Yontif (holiday) 52
23. Snowbirds Fly North for Passover 54
24. Don't Run…Walk 56
25. "Whose Sock is This Anyway?" 60
26. Do Jewish Girls Really Camp Out? 62
27. Time to Move to Florida… Time to Sell our House up North…....................................... 64

28.	Downsizing	66
29.	Take Me, I'm Free	68
30.	The Location was "To Die For"… the Interior of the House, "Oy !"	70

Holidays

31.	Which Menorah Should We Use This Year?	75
32.	Is It Early or Late This Year?	77
33.	Another Look at the Holiday	80
34.	It's an Eating Marathon	82
35.	Blintzes for Break the Fast	84
36.	Let's Discuss the High Holidays…	86
37.	Where's a Good Chinese Restaurant?	88
38.	Chanukah is Around the Corner	91
39.	"Jew Year Resolutions"	93
40.	My first Passover in Florida…	95
41.	Whose House this Year?	97
42.	Small Plane Travel is Not for This Jewish Mother	99
43.	You Call This a Vacation?	101
44.	"I Need a Vacation after a Vacation"	104
45.	I Travel with Two Dresses	106
46.	"A Walk and a Half"	109

The Children

47.	Here Come the Children!!!!!!!	113
48.	My Children Trust Me with their House Keys	116
49.	'Hak mir nit kain tcheinik'	118
50.	"Kislev was Good to Me"	120
51.	"Call Me When You Get There"	123
52.	"Tell Me After"	125
53.	Matchmaker, Matchmaker, Make <u>Him</u> a Match…	127
54.	Grandmas No Longer Have Blue Hair	129
55.	Being a Grandmother Beats Being a Mother	131
56.	This Is Retirement?	133
57.	Living in an Active Adult Community	133
58.	"Fill 'er Up?"	135

59.	The BocaYente Attended an Eastern Star Installation	137
60.	I Don't Recognize these People	139
61.	This is Dinner Conversation?	141
62.	We Did a Mitzvah for the Children	143
63.	Welcome to the Neighborhood	145
64.	It's Flu Season Again	147
65.	Jewish.com	149
66.	Cooking with Phyllis	151
67.	The Infamous Junk Drawer	153
68.	Where's that Sock?	155
69.	Certain Tasks Only a Woman Can Perform	157
70.	I Remember When…	160
71.	Have You Ever Been to a "Jewish Pot Luck Dinner?"	162
72.	This is a Security Guard?	164
73.	E-mailing Has Become a Way of Life for Some People	166

Serious Ramblings of the Boca Yente

74.	The Totem Pole of Priorities	171
75.	A Lovely Place to Be	173
76.	The Air is Heavy in a Waiting Room	176
77.	Listen to Us Once in a While	179
78.	I Can Travel… Alone	181
79.	Time to Visit the Folks	184
80.	Home is Where the Mezuzah is	186
81.	My Favorite Story Originally Written 1978	188
82.	"Let Me Tell You About My Affair"	188
83.	The Day of the Twilight Bar Mitzvah	191

The Birth of the BocaYente

I am the BocaYente.

I was *conceived* in January, 1998. My parents were a computer and a sense of humor.

In my embryonic years, I was an active parent of two sons, wife of a periodontist, and devoted daughter to a Jewish mother and father. As I matured, I was a very inquisitive child and observed everyone around me. I noted the behavior of adults in different social situations and turned them into comic entertainment.

I was *born* a *Snowbird* in January, 1999, in sunny southern Florida, immediately following my husband's retirement. *(A Snowbird is a resident of a northern state who only resides in Florida for three or four months of the winter season.)* After my birth, I found time to write and I sat down at the computer and penned humorous e-mails to my friends and family. The friends and family began to forward these comical essays to others and the distribution list grew every day.

I became the yenta of Boca, The BocaYente.

The e-mails were such a success that the *North Shore Jewish Journal* of Salem, Massachusetts, invited the **BocaYente** to become a featured columnist. I joined the staff in 2002 and penned a column titled, *A Slice of Life.*

Presently, along with speaking engagements, I am a guest columnist at the *Journal*. I decided to collate all the articles and publish this edition of ***The BocaYente's Slice of Life***.

Within these covers are not only humorous essays, but thought-provoking and sensitive articles written by the **BocaYente**. You will "feel for me" when I sell my house full of *stuff*. You will know my joy when I become a grandmother. You will have hot flashes with me, and I am sure you will enjoy the discussions with my husband, Jerry, who enjoys retirement and has selective hearing when it comes to listening to me.

Hopefully, you will love ***The BocaYente's Slice of Life*** because I am the **BocaYente**.

Prologue: It is important to understand the migration of the Jewish people to the land of sunshine, sunny Florida, USA...

The Lost Tribes of Israel

There were twelve tribes of Israel. Two tribes, we know, settled in the south of Canaan, and ten tribes settled in the north. In 722 BCE, Israel lost track of ten of its tribes. No written word in history books could ever explain the disappearance of the Ten Lost Tribes of Israel.

Each leader of the twelve tribes was a son of Jacob. Can you imagine twelve brothers getting along? It just didn't work. They had to separate and move away from one another. The wives of the brothers were at each other's throats all the time and driving them crazy.

You can imagine the women saying, *"Nu, so look at your brother's wife. She has a bigger tent than I do and has more jewels on her fingers. I should have married your brother."*

The brothers decided they couldn't stand the *tumult* (confusion) and the *kvetching* (complaining) of the wives any longer so they would move away from one another, but they would try to keep in touch.

Ten brothers went north; two went south. The trials and tribulations of the two tribes that went south remain in our history books. The other ten tribes' saga is a mystery.

I have a theory

The ten tribes from the north had a meeting and decided it was too cold to stay up north, so they trekked down to the south and established a new homeland. They called it Florida.

It was a state of golden sunshine, a land of milk and honey. It was warm there. Everyone was Jewish. They ate three meals a day. They ate dinner early in the evening so they could get a good night's sleep and could eliminate the need for driving at night.

There were orange groves nearby; they could send grapefruit and oranges in the winter months to their relatives in other tribes. There were other natives living there from distant lands who were available to clean their tents for a minimum of wages; and the weather was always beautiful...maybe, a little hot at times, but not so terrible.

They had hairdressers and manicurists and clubhouses with activities so they could all play together. It was the Promised Land.

So what do you think happened?

Word got out. *Lantzmen* (relatives) from all over the country heard about this new Jewish Homeland. They started arriving in droves and in big Lincolns and Lexuses, and they all spoke with different accents. They were from the Land of the northeast: New York, New Jersey, Philadelphia, Connecticut, and Boston. No one was from Wyoming or Idaho. The ten tribes began to adopt the customs of these newcomers.

For instance, the New Yorkers introduced the others to delicatessen, big corned beef sandwiches, and to cheese cake, big thick creamy slices, and to bagels. Bagels were made from round pieces of dough with holes in them. Incidentally, gentiles just discovered bagels within the past ten years.

The people from Philadelphia introduced the others to cream cheese; and *nu*, there was a match: bagels and Philadelphia cream cheese.

The Bostonians tried to teach the other *lantzmen* the King's English and proper diction, but the others could never learn how to say "cahr" correctly or to speak without an accent. They did learn to like Boston baked beans.

The people from New Jersey taught the others how to build long roads. They said they had a very long road in New Jersey that allowed transportation to flow smoothly. The idea was adopted and called a turnpike. These turnpikes today are sometimes considered parking lots.

The tribesmen from Connecticut tried to convince the other tribal members to open a gambling casino. They believed they could make a great deal of money. However, the Jews frowned upon gambling and decided to let another tribe come along someday and make a go of that idea. Oy, did the Jews miss an opportunity then. Another tribe did just that, and they are making lots of wampum today in Connecticut.

This is how Florida was begat. Floridians are descendants of the ten tribes of Israel. We are not lost anymore. We are *fahrmished (*confused) at times, but we are not lost. We all live happily ever after.

When the BocaYente first moved to Florida as a Snowbird, she rented in an apartment complex. The following articles reflect those winter months...

Our First Apartment in Florida

We found a nice unit in a lovely apartment house, and we signed a lease for three months. It is centrally located between Costco's and Bloomingdale's. What more could I ask?

I've decided that Jerry and I are probably the oldest tenants in this complex. Most of the tenants are young working adults or college students. We are the *alta kakas* (old people).

It's been a long time since I've lived in an apartment house. I have decided that the two young men in the top apartment must be deaf because they play their stereo at an ear-splitting volume. Thank G-d, I haven't had a headache while they were listening to their music or I would have gone ballistic. I can't believe I'm even referring to *that noise* as music.

You see, they have a sub-woofer. A sub-woofer is a bass speaker. They have that sub-woofer turned up to the limit. I do not believe any living being can hear the melody; they can only hear and feel the bass vibrations. There were times my heart was beating in time with the sounds of the bass emanating from the bass sub-woofer.

When these two young men greet me and ask, "How's it goin'?" I just smile. I assume they must be hearing-impaired, and I don't know sign language to answer their greeting. I do know a sign I could give to them; however, when I went to *"flip it,"* I mean, sign it, Jerry, my husband, told me it wasn't lady-like and not to make that gesture.

When you live in an apartment, you smell cooking, right? <u>Not in Florida</u>. No one eats in! Not even these young kids. So, no smell of food. Once, I did smell something sweet and when I commented on the pleasant odor, Jerry smiled and said, *"That's not perfume or food."* Did you figure it out? Right! *Grass...* and not the kind that you find growing in the front yard.

We rented on the first floor since there is no elevator in this three-story building. Who can walk up two or three flights of stairs at this age without stopping at every floor to use an inhaler?

Although, would it be better to live in an apartment house with *older* people? Does "Meals on Wheels" have such a pleasant odor? Would it be different to hear a television blaring away because the tenants *really* are deaf? And, isn't it great to see young people taking those stairs two at a time to reach the third floor?

It brings back memories...days when we were younger, when we could take the stairs two at a time.

I Was the Only One Wearing a One-Piece Bathing Suit

Today I had a most unsettling experience. The day started as usual. Jerry and I began the morning by taking a 25-minute walk, worked out in the gym, ate breakfast and read the newspaper. I did some errands, and Jerry went "on the computer" to check our stock holdings. Mid-day we had lunch together and then decided to sit at the pool for a while to read and enjoy the sun.

I will preface the following remarks by telling you we live in a *young* apartment complex...not an *alta-kaka* complex that comes to mind when you think of Florida. Twenty and thirty-year-old working people live here, with a few old-timers thrown in, like us.

Well, let me tell you what an eye-opener we had. Jerry did not know where to look first. To reach the chairs we wanted to sit in, we had to walk around a girl, lying on a chaise lounge, with her "bosooms" hanging down below her armpits. Jerry almost fell in the pool since he was not looking where he was going.

I was the ONLY ONE with a one-piece bathing suit. Jerry was the ONLY ONE wearing a hat and sneakers and socks.

The guys wore sandals or loafers with no socks. The girls wore strings around their breasts, and patches and strings of material over you-know-what else. The girls walked around with constant wedgies.

After the novelty of "people-watching" wore off, Jerry fell asleep and naturally snored with his mouth open. I read my novel and snoozed a little too. We sauntered away feeling 110 years old.

The moral of the story is: Been there, done that. Life goes on...

School at my Age?

Today I went to my first Bonsai class at the Morakami Gardens. I loved it.

Bonsai, by the way, is pronounced, "bones-eye." Bonsai is the art of creating an artistic representation of a mature tree in nature. The planter, the soil, the trunk of the tree is all part of the creation. It is a Japanese art form.

There are ten people in my class. One man has four strands of hair growing only in the back of his head, and he has those strands tied in a miniature pony tail. He is about 65, sitting with his cell phone attached to his belt in case he is called to the E.R. for emergency brain surgery.....right!!!

The young man next to me has a bigger diamond stud in his ear than I have on my wedding ring. He is very nice and invited me to lunch.

The instructor was very nice and good looking, to boot. I'd guess he's about 65 years old. Sixty-five is young to me already. At one point, Dick, the instructor's name, not his "appendage," was cutting the branches so much I thought nothing would be left on the trunk. He asked what the class thought. Not being the shy type, I told him I was glad he was not my hair dresser. He didn't think my remark was very funny.

The class lasted about two hours. After an hour and a half, I said to the guy next to me, *"Evidently, he does not have a prostate problem because my bladder is going to burst, and I am starving from smelling the cooking aromas of the food in the restaurant."* That's when "Diamond earring" or "Stud" fell in love with me and invited me for lunch with him. I'm not his type except we're both Jewish. Did I mention eight out of ten were of the "Jewish persuasion?" We actually go on a field trip to a nursery (not a children's nursery, but a plant nursery). We make our own bonsai trees with wires and potting soil. Then we artistically trim the trees. Good-bye manicure!!

It was two hours that Jerry and I spent away from one another. I guess we're not attached at the hip, after all. I've decided that separation, *temporary* separation, is very healthy when both husband and wife are retired. Actually, the scary thing is, we haven't minded being together at all.

This is the first adult learning course I've taken in Florida, and I realize there is so much out there for me to discover and learn. I finally grew tired of talking about taking classes and decided it was time to act upon my words and thoughts. I realize that now is the time to take advantage of all these available courses and interesting events. I have no excuse. I have the time, and I'm going to use the time.

Sayonara until the next class.

"Can You Hear Me? Can You Hear Me Now?"

Today Jerry went to have a hearing test. I am tired of his saying, *"I never heard you say that."* I swear he has selective hearing, like all men. They hear what they want to hear. For years, he claimed he had a hearing loss. Whenever he forgot to do something or to go somewhere, he'd say, *"I never heard you say that."*

"Of course, I told you," I would answer.

"I don't remember you ever telling me."

Now I ask him, *"Which is it? You never heard me or you don't remember? Is your hearing going or is your memory fading? Do you need a hearing aid or ginko biloba to improve your memory?"*

I take the vitamin, ginko biloba, to improve my memory…when I remember where I put the bottle.

I decided to make an appointment for Jerry with an audiologist for a hearing test. Would you believe he **forgot** the appointment? So help me, he forgot it. He reappointed the time for the following week. He returned very sheepishly after the test and was almost afraid to tell me the results.

I asked, *"The testing was negative, right? You hear perfectly? All the decibel sounds…you have no hearing loss."*

*"Yes, on all those counts. I figured out that I hear what I want to hear, and sometimes what you tell me isn't important to me so **I half listen and then forget that half**. I compartmentalize what's important and what's not important."*

"In other words, what I say isn't important to you?"

"Well, sometimes," he answered.

Do you know how he regretted those words when they were out of his mouth? He knew he should have lied rather than speak the truth. He actually wished he had come home and told me he was "Stone Deaf."

Today I don't worry whether he can hear or not. I stopped talking to him.

Truthfully, I think he planned this strategy and had his prayers answered.

That "son-of-a-gun," I'm going to start talking to him again.

The Eye of the Needle

When was the last time you threaded a needle?

I began the ordeal last week. I finished this week.

I never remember where I keep the needle and thread. It has been so long since I did any sewing; and, mind you, when I say sewing, I mean sewing a button on a shirt. I do not mean "making" a dress from a pattern. The last and *only* time I made a dress was in Junior High School sewing class, and I almost failed the course.

Remember when you had to wear to school the skirt or dress you made from a pattern? I begged my mother to let me skip school that day. Oh, I was so embarrassed to walk around classes in that skirt that was hemmed up to my knees in the front and down to the floor in the back. *Oy*, I remember it so vividly.

I had to dig deep into the recesses of my mind and say, "*O.k., if you were a sewing kit, where would you be?*" I rummaged through two hundred drawers, looking under and over every single item and checking every closet until I found the sewing kit on a shelf in the bathroom linen closet where it is usually kept.

I must now thread the needle. I choose the needle with the biggest loop at the head and break off a piece of thread. Of course, I should have cut the thread with a scissors to make it easier, but G-d forbid, I should get up again and look for a scissors. You realize that I eventually have to get up and find the scissors, don't you?

I begin by holding up the needle, sitting and facing the light coming through the window pane, and I attempt to push the thread through the needle. **Every single time** I begin to insert the thread through the hole, one strand of thread breaks loose from the main "stem" and pushes away from the side of the needle.

And I can't decide whether I should look through the ***top*** of my bifocals, the ***bottom*** of my bifocals, or remove my glasses altogether.

I try to thread the needle straight on, sidewards, everywaywards. I put the thread in my mouth to dampen it, to make it easier to loop. Now it's wet, and it still goes nowhere except off the side of the needle.

I am now on the verge of throwing the shirt away and buying a new one that has all the buttons intact.

"*Once more,*" I say to myself, and I try to thread the needle again.

Hoo-ha, I did it.

All the instructions I learned in my seventh grade sewing class lessons flood my memory banks, and I actually do a fine job of sewing the button on the shirt...until the end when I must "finish off."

I go back and forth and make a knot...and ***just*** when I'm ready to cut the remaining piece of thread, a *loop* of thread appears from nowhere, and the thread becomes knotted up.

"*&#*", I say aloud. I don't care who hears or sees me at this point. It's been three days since I have moved from the kitchen chair, and I am determined to finish sewing this *farshtunkina* button on the shirt.

If I cut the loop of thread, I run the risk of ruining the knot; if I sew the loop under the back of the button somehow, it may hold, but will it show?

I could care less at this point. Somehow, I manage to make the final knot, and I never want to see this shirt again; never mind, wear it.

When I was a little girl, I remember my mother always asked me if I would thread the needle for her, and I could never understand why she couldn't do it herself.

Today I understand. I have no little girl to ask to help me. I only have a middle-aged husband who sees even worse than I do. So......it just takes me a little longer to do it myself!!!!!

A Hot Flash is a Gender Discriminatory Action

Words cannot do justice to describing a woman in the throes of a hot flash. Perhaps, if you visualize a volcano erupting and spilling lava and compare that to a woman experiencing a fire within her body and her erupting and perspiring to alleviate the inferno, you may understand the problem.

You must witness a woman "having a hot flash" to even understand the suffering she endures during this episode. There are certain *signals* that alert the observer to a woman experiencing a hot flash.

The face of a woman becomes "beet-red," her hands pull and stretch the neck of her turtleneck sweater and then she rips it off her body. Her eyeglasses fly to the other side of the room, her earrings rip her pierced ear lobes while she is pulling off her sweater, and she is **unaware** of her surroundings.

She is suffering at this point in time, and she is almost in a catatonic state.

Make-up is dripping down and under her chin, eye liner is sliding down her cheek, and she is using the sleeve of her white silk blouse to wipe her face with no regard for the garment. She is ON FIRE and she is MELTING. The heat within her is more intense than the heat of a sauna, the steam from a boiler room, or the rays of a desert sun. It begins within the chest wall of the woman and escapes from every pore and cavity of her body.

There are no warning signs when the assault will begin. No amount of cold water or cool air can arrest the eruption. The attack on her body persists for minutes that seem like hours. During a twenty-four-hour period, there can be one attack, two attacks, or as many as twenty attacks upon her.

Following the attack upon her body, she now has to acclimate herself to her normal body temperature and she now becomes *chilled* by the perspiration accumulated on her skin. She shivers and shakes. Her clothes are soaking wet. Her hair is soaked and sticking to her forehead and to the back of her neck. This hot flash renders her physically and *emotionally* exhausted. She becomes irritated and irritating. Her mind cannot function. She has no patience for others, and she can not make rational decisions.

She lives in fear of the next attack. She suffers anxiety wondering when and where the next flash will occur. Thoughts go around in her mind: *Will she be alone when she suffers the next attack? Will people watch her as she gyrates and strips off her clothes and evolves into another personality? Will she be pitied? Laughed at? Shunned? Ostracized? Recognized?*

It is so unfair to Woman. As a teenager, she menstruates and has cramps. As a young woman she endures labor pains and gives birth. And then in her mature years, when she could enjoy life and not worry about conception, she must now tolerate menopause.

Menopause is women's enemy. There is no justification in the fact that with all the sweating during a hot flash, **women do not lose one pound**…just the opposite. Women usually gain weight.

A hot flash is discriminatory by gender. It only attacks women.

Where's *N.O.W.* when you need them?

Sshh…Don't Talk About It……

When we reach the age of fifty, we must consider undergoing certain health procedures. We do not like to speak aloud of these specific tests. We whisper them to our friends and ask their opinion. The details of the tests are not exactly topics for dinner conversations.

One of the tests is the good-old colonoscopy which we should all have at the age of fifty and have repeated every five years; as if once wasn't enough for this invasive violation of our body.

Women are used to the pap smear and the mammogram, but the colonoscopy is a different story. The procedure is like an invasion from outer space. It is executed with a wand that is as long as our imagination. This "magic" wand invades our colon; and our colon is 5 feet long and twisted like a noodle. How does that "magic" instrument with the headlight go around the intestinal curves?

The doctors insist that this is a necessary test at our age, so we schedule the date months ahead from the date of procedure. From that day on, we lose precious hours of sleep. We toss and turn thinking about the upcoming event. We imagine the worst. We suffer anxious moments. We even have night sweats. We have not heard horrible stories about the actual colonoscopy. We have heard the "war stories" of the day and night <u>before </u>the procedure.

We must swallow a drink from *Sugar Hell* that promises to reduce our weight by 2 lbs. within hours. Of course, the *how* of the weight loss is beyond words. We begin the night before by drinking 8 oz. of this incredibly sweet, disgusting drink, and say, *"Hey, that wasn't so bad."* We follow with a chaser of water at ten in the evening and hit the sack.

That's all we do...is **hit** the sack. We never sleep. We now run to the bathroom every fifteen minutes and spend the late evening and early morning hours on the "hopper." We cannot exit the bathroom, nor do we even consider the thought of leaving the throne. We have no strength.

In the morning we must arise from our "seat" and shower and dress and go to the hospital for the test. With all the strength we can muster, we drag ourselves to the car and ask spouse or friend to drive us to the hospital. We are not allowed to do it for ourselves...as if we even have the strength to press the accelerator. We take no reading material for the hospital. We have already read three novels during our early morning vigil in the bathroom.

We arrive at the Outpatient Clinic in our anorexic condition, and they have us undress (we've just dressed) and get on a gurney. We are wheeled into a room where there is a screen before us so that we can watch the *"Journey of the Colonoscope."* The nurse injects us with intravenous valium, and the journey begins for them and for us. We, the patients, are in "twilight zone," and occasionally, some of us sleep, thank G-d. The doctors watch the screen, we hope.

Within the hour, we are awakened, told we can go home, and have accomplished one more step recommended by AARP.

The best thing: we've lost weight.

The worst thing: the weight returns the very next day, and the test has to be repeated in another 5 years!!

Vanity, Thy Name is Woman

The BocaYente put on a few extra pounds this winter due to the fact that the city of Boca has over 500 restaurants and each one is wonderful. The BocaYente, naturally, had to try each and every delicacy of each and every restaurant. The majority of them passed my standards with flying colors and left me with a project for the summer...to shed some weight.

In the summer, dieting is not an easy task because licking ice cream is a very nice treat on a hot night, and drinking an ice-cold beer is really thirst-quenching on a hot day. But I made up my mind a week ago to shed some weight, and I have been really good.

Every night I have for dinner one protein and two vegetables. **Do you know how boring this is?** No pasta, no wonderful baked potato with soured cream, no bread, no rice. Added to this decision of losing weight in my life-style, I am now working with an exercise trainer to *solidify* my "few" extra pounds.

When I see the trainer approaching my home for our weekly sessions, I lock the door and tell her the occupants of this residence have moved. She seems to know it's my voice, has yet to believe me and continues to ring the bell. She weighs about 90 lbs., lifts weights of 100 lbs. and makes me feel like "Kate Smith", for those of you who remember Kate Smith.

She looks like Kate Moss. *Two different-size Kates in one room.*

We begin by stretching. I start to perspire. *"O.k., I've stretched enough."* Now we work with weights. She's smiling, speaking words of encouragement, and I am secretly wishing her disappearance from the room.

Sit-up time....oh my G-d. My stomach feels like an accordion with rows of fat squeezing together and looking like a wave formation. The Torturer, my pet name for my trainer, puts a huge ball between my legs for me to squeeze so as to reduce the blubber on the inside of my thighs and to eradicate the number one killer, **Cellulite.** At this point in the routine, I am contemplating wearing long pants for the rest of the summer and skipping this tortuous routine.

We end the session with her saying, *"Don't you feel better now for doing these routines?"*

"NO, I feel like sh*#" is what I want to say.

I just smile and say, *"Oh, I certainly do."* Right!!

I am smiling because she's leaving. I am considering resting on my bed for *just* a few minutes, but if I lie down for a few minutes, I'll never get up again until tomorrow morning, and the next day is the **Killer Day.** I will feel muscles I never knew I had. They will be on fire and I will want to scream, *"Advil, my Advil, where are you?"*

I will turn my bathroom apart looking for pain killers, and I will walk like a ballerina. I will be unable to climb stairs. I will be crippled. I will be unable to open a jar or pick up anything from the floor. My arms won't bend, and my legs won't move.

I don't know, Ladies. Is it worth it? To lose a few pounds? Oh, I know all the health benefits, but give me a break. Who's doing this for their health? **Vanity, thy name is Woman.**

Cellulite is America's Number One Most Wanted Enemy

Posters hang on refrigerator doors in homes throughout the country. Photos of round irregular fat cells have been indelibly stamped in our minds, subliminally stored so its image appears wherever we go...in dark corners, theatres, hallways, restaurants, toilets, everywhere.

YET every magazine has a gorgeous model on the cover with not one ounce of extra fat on her body. She is lean, tanned, architecturally sound, with skin as smooth as silk.

I've been known to draw moustaches on these magazine cover models; and, at times, I have had to withstrain myself from destroying entire magazine racks. In supermarkets, waiting my turn in line at the check-out corner with groceries loaded in my shopping cart, I should not have to be subjected to the painful ordeal of staring at beautiful young women on the covers of magazines. Where is their cellulite?

I am a Bounty Hunter. I go after Cellulite. I am my first client. I would like to tell you of my adventures in capturing Public Enemy Number One using the weapons of fruits and vegetables, vitamins, healthy foods, such as tofu which still makes me shiver, and exercise.

I decided to make jogging my first venture in destroying my cellulite. In the evening before bedtime, I set my alarm for 5:30 a.m. I never knew there was a five thirty in the *morning*. The alarm rang at the appointed hour the following day. I immediately hit the snooze alarm. There was no way my body could move at that time. I finally managed to get up at seven in the morning. Do you know it is pitch dark at 5:30 a.m., and it is cold outside in the fall and winter, and it's not so wonderful at 7:00 a.m. either?

I realize other people run at that hour. My sister does it every morning. She runs in the dark and cold for three miles.

Secretly, I've always felt she had a morning paper route to get up at that hour. Why else would she run around town in the dark? She was probably too embarrassed to tell the rest of the family she needed the money.

I managed to get out of bed, and I left my husband snoring away. I put on my $150 pair of sneakers that I was told were essential for "serious" runners, my $500 running uniform with orange reflectors so that no car should mistake me for a tree and slam into me; or a dog, G-d forbid, should mistake me for a tree and empty his bladder. I was not ruining this outfit. I strapped my Walkman around my waist and was ready to go. My outfit cost as much as my mortgage payment.

I stepped out the front door, key around my wrist in a special wrist-pac, walked down the front path, and began doing warm-ups. I looked around, hoping my neighbors would see how athletic and color-coordinated I looked, but everyone must have been sleeping at that hour. I stretched my calf muscles, my ankle joints, and moved my head loosely in a rotating direction. Actually, I think I gave myself whiplash.

I began my run.

I ran...and ran...and ran...and made it to the sixth house from mine. I was panting, my face was flushed, my legs were on fire, and my throat was parched. My heart was beating faster and louder than the *1812 Overture*. My outfit looked nice, though. I thought I was dying. I kept thinking about my sister who ran three miles daily. Who was she really? Wonder Woman? I began to respect her. I mean, she was my *older* sister. I just hope she doesn't take up gourmet cooking. I'll secretly compete and end up looking like a blimp and burn my house down.

When I left the house early in the morning looking fit and adorable, no one was to be seen. Now that I am sweating and exhausted from trying to run, the garage doors on my street are all open, and my neighbors are standing there smiling. I never see half these people throughout the year. Now they are there, each and every one of them, standing on the street watching like it was a parade route, and I was the "float."

Jogging was out. I decided to try exercising.

I began at home in the private confines of my den which I had converted to an exercise room, or should I say, torture chamber. I purchased a Nordic Track, television, stereo, ab-roller, and barbells ranging from three-pound weights to ten-pound weights. I had to take out a loan to equip this room, but I was not leaving the house and going to a public or private gym and strut in front of a long mirror flexing invisible muscles. I was also not going to get into one of those spandex numbers in public. Those outfits accentuate every bulge in your body and come in every bright color imaginable. What happened to basic black?

In the den I began by placing an exercise tape in my VCR and following along with the instructor who was as thin as a pretzel. I jumped. I twisted. I grunted. I groaned. I moved my left arm up, my right arm up. I did jumping jacks. I pointed my toes to the heaven, my thighs to the sky. I bent forward, backward, sideways. I twisted my body as if it were rubber, in ways it never dreamed it could be positioned. My husband should be so lucky to see me move like this.

My heart was beating as if it were going to burst from my chest wall. My ribs were slowly detaching from my spinal column. I was disintegrating as a human body cell within minutes. I began to smell odors in the room. I looked around for the source. It was **me**. My clothes couldn't stand me and even wanted to walk away without me in it. The outfit needed an airing. No, it needed a burning. I was disgusting. I smelled like a gymnasium...an entire gymnasium. I crawled over to the remote control and stopped the videotape in midstream. Actually, I wanted to throw the remote control through the screen. I rested on the floor mat (which I was told was necessary equipment), and decided that was it for the exercise tape today.

I would try the ab-roller. Maybe I would like that better.

I lie down on my back, situated myself under the pretty purple ab-roller that I had purchased one night at three in the morning when I couldn't sleep and saw it on an informmercial. That, in itself, should have told me something. I put my hands on the sides of the contraption, took a deep breath to roll myself up and watch my waistline disappear. I pulled. I pulled again. I didn't budge. All right, let's try this again...deep breath, exert the strength in the arms and pull up.

I did it.

I actually felt an air pocket between the floor and my back. Should I try again? I was on a roll. I decided that was enough of that for the first time. I rationalized more in that space of time for putting a halt to working the ab-roller than anyone would have believed possible. On to the Nordic Track. That *could* be tricky.

In the store, the salesman said to move the left foot in time with the right arm... just like you walk.

How the hell do the salespeople walk? I felt like a dysfunctional individual with a coordination problem. I went flying off the track three times. My arms were going wherever they wanted and whenever they wanted. My feet were in coordination with nothing, maybe the floorboards. This was not going to be easy. I had better try something else.

The weights...

Stupid, I'm not. I had to end this session on an up-note. I decided to use three-pound weights. Up and down, up and down, down and up, down and up. That's it. Four reps, sounds good to me. I mastered it. I'm quitting for the day (or forever).

I'm going shopping for a size smaller in my clothes. This cellulite was just going to melt off my body. I could feel it.

Actually, that's not what I was feeling, but the agony that was beginning to permeate through my body made me believe I had been successful and that I had lost inches within that time span.

I crawled up the stairs, into the shower, donned my robe, and layed down on my bed for just a few moments. I awoke six hours later at dinner time. I tried to get off the bed, but I knew that while sleeping, a truck had come into my house and rolled over me. My legs were cramped and situated in an unusual position, my arms were immobile, and I was contemplating euthanasia...if I had the strength.

I was a failure at running. I hated exercising but, I hated my cellulite problem even more. I wanted to look like one of those women on the covers of the magazines.

The solution to my problem came to me like a flash. I would sell all the equipment and my running apparatus at a yard sale and use the proceeds for a worthy cause.

I would have Liposuction!!

Welcome College Alumni

Today, in the mail, I received an invitation to my Sorority College Reunion. I was so excited. I was going to see my sorority sisters whom I haven't seen in years.

I began to plan my wardrobe, my means of transportation, and then **Panic** set in.

I weighed less than 100 lbs. in college. I certainly don't weigh in at that number anymore. My hair was brown with blond frosting. It's still brown with blond frosting, only the roots are gray, **and** "only my hairdresser knows for sure" my color mixture.

I wore contact lenses in college. I wear bifocals now. I was 5'6" in my younger years. I'm only 5' now. Well, maybe I wasn't 5'6". *I always wished I were*.

I could run up a flight of stairs like a flash, could move heavy items, and I could walk into downtown Amherst from my sorority house which was two miles away and still feel fine…no racing heartbeat or huffing and puffing. I could fly faster than a speeding bullet, was stronger than a speeding train and jumped over tall buildings with a single bound…OK, I'm exaggerating a little now!!

I hardly wore makeup during the day, maybe a base and some lipstick. Now I put pounds of base and powder on to fill in the wrinkles. I was young and single. Today I'm middle-aged, and I'm a grandmother.

What happened? Where did those days go?

Today I walk up a flight of stairs, and on the third stair I am already huffing and puffing. I have to catch my breath on the landing, and that's only ten steps from the beginning. I can't move a chair without "pulling out my back."

I play tennis looking like I'm going to war. I have a support on my arm for "tennis elbow," a support for my knee, and a sweatband on my wrist. I'm an advertisement for orthopedic fittings; although, I will admit I have nice tennis outfits.

I don't walk to town. I drive. When I finish driving and doing my errands, I read a book and fall asleep, and it's only the middle of the day. I wear make-up in the morning, in the afternoon, evening, and to bed. I don't need to look at the lines in my face, the dark color under my eyes, and the liver spots on my cheeks.

How can I go to the reunion looking like this? I immediately telephoned my trainer.

"HELP! We need to do overtime. I have to lose 95 lbs., get taller, and I need a facelift in three weeks time. What do you think?"

She hung up on me.

I called back. "*Help!*"

"Phyllis, are you nuts? I'm a trainer, not a magician or a plastic surgeon. I can work you harder on your exercises, but then you're liable to pull out your back. And, do you want your jaws wired shut to curb your eating habits... which aren't exactly the best anyway?"

"How can I go to my reunion?"

"Do you really have to worry about how you look at the reunion? Your friends are going to look different too, you know. Maybe they won't even look at you and just remember all your good points as a student?"

"I don't think so. I was an 'itch.' I pulled practical jokes, and I was so thin that I looked like a refugee, so everyone

hated me for being thin when they were already counting calories. It just took me twenty years to catch up."

"Phyllis, you know what? After hearing all this, why don't you stay home?"

"But Jerry's retired, and it will be another night of his reading and watching TV and my reading a book or working on a bonsai plant. **Screw it!** *I am going to this reunion. It beats the alternative of staying home. I can still drive at night."*

At this point in time, I am breaking my neck with an exercise trainer, trying to get a little tan to blend with my wrinkles, making a hair appointment, facial and manicure for that day, and I am planning to wear the "smartest" designer outfit in my closet…or perhaps, I may buy a *little* outfit.

I am going to make my sorority sisters hate me all over again…only with envy. And the truth is, I can't wait to go, and I don't care how I or anyone looks. These were my "sisters, "my "buddies." I lived with them in the same sorority house for over two years. We shared secret ceremonial *mishagas* (craziness). We lived in *shmootz* (dirt) some days. We studied, laughed and cried together.

I can't wait to hear about their lives and to share stories of my life. Some of my old friends won't be there because they live far away. Others won't be there because they passed away. They will be missed. G-d willing, I'm not missing it.

Tennis Warriors

I play tennis with a tough group in my community. In fact, each and every tennis player is tough.

Tennis players are Warriors. They are easily identified by their armor. They are bandaged from head to toe. Most of the men and women wear armor right below their elbow. The armament is beige-colored and elasticized. It is an ace bandage support needed for tennis elbow.

Some male warriors wear armor around their knee. It is black, elasticized and has an opening for the knee cap. That is an athletic support for the knees. Other warriors wear white around their forehead, perhaps, to identify their tribe; and, still others wear white around their wrists to absorb the perspiration accumulated during battle.

Some women wear hats with holes on top to aerate their scalps during high noon, and the men wear baseball caps with *no* holes. They have no hair to aerate. A few warriors wear their caps backwards. They are making a statement, *"I do not want you to see the back of my neck."*

I play with a tribe whose antics are typical of a normal skirmish on the battlefield of tennis. We begin by doing a tribal dance. We jump around on each foot and stare at our enemy across the cloth divide. One warrior, the first warrior, holds the racquet-weapon in one hand and the yellow ammo-ball in the other hand. She stands at the edge of the battlefield, bounces the yellow ammunition on the ground to test available explosive power. She stares at her enemy, again looks down at the bouncing yellow ammo, and extends her arm holding the weapon. She does this act once, twice, winding up, and then smacks the yellow ammo at the enemy on the other side of the cloth divide.

All the warriors now shift from one leg to another and follow the flight of the yellow ammo. The initial warrior is catatonic due to serving the ammo. She has pain radiating up the arm strapped with the protective elbow support, but she does not want the other warriors to see her physical discomfort. She suffers silently although she is praying her arm will fall off at this point and rid her of the shooting pain.

Some warriors **run** to return the ammo, others **limp** to the ammo, and others **stand** there and wait for the ammo to come to them. Some begin running and end up limping due to a common tennis injury called a "groin pull." Ooh, that hurts, and you can't hold that painful area or rub it on the battlefield or you will be thrown off the court for indecent behavior.

We dance our tribal side-step, shout our tribal obscenities, sign tribal hand and finger gestures when truly aggravated.

We are Tennis Warriors. We can withstand pain. We wear our armament with pride…our tennis elbow supports, our knee supports, our sweatbands, our leg braces that bend because… **We love our tennis.**

What Your Car Says About You

Is your car a reflection of you?

What motivated you to buy the car that you are driving? Finances? Fantasy? Your spouse suggested it? It is recommended by *Consumer Reports*...?

Cars are indicators of personalities. There are sport cars for age-defying middle-aged men and women, minivans for soccer moms, sedans for the conservative folk and SUV's for the young suburbanites.

Janet Reno drives a red truck...a pick-up truck. "*A truck enhances feelings of masculinity*," says Dr. Charles Kenny, a psychologist and president of consumer psychology firm, Kenny & Associates.

Television ads portray the owners of SUV's as adventurous travelers. They can climb mountains (there are none in Florida except for land-fills), ford streams (our lakes and canals?) and can travel anywhere. In actuality, the SUV, in Florida, is used mainly by snowbirds *shlepping* clothes back and forth from Boston and New York to Florida.

A large number of people in Florida drive Lincoln Town cars. Wow, that is one big vehicle! The front end of the car is in Florida and the rear end is in Georgia. Most drivers of Lincoln Town cars view the road through the opening of the steering wheel...right below the rim, and only drive in the left hand lane. I go out of my way to avoid a Lincoln Town Car; especially, in a parking lot. They all seem to back out of their parking spaces at the same time.

There are popular upscale cars found in Florida such as the Lexus, Mercedes, BMW, to name a few. These cars usually have tinted windows and shiny wheels. The driver of these cars is a mystery. Who can see anyone through the tinted windows?

I, myself, am very fond of the Jaguar. The female driver of a Jaguar always has blonde hair, wears sunglasses (even at night) and has a Rolex watch on her left hand while holding on to the side view mirror.

The male driver has either one beautiful mane of dark wavy hair or is bald as a cueball. He, too, wears the standard Rolex watch and sunglasses as well.

I drive a convertible. When the sun comes out, I put the top down (top of the car, that is) and drive with the wind blowing through my hair. I am twenty-one all over again. That's how I feel at the time. I don't feel that way when I wake in the morning. In the morning I wonder which part of my body is going to ache. But, put me in the driver's seat, and I am twenty-one all over again.

So why did you choose the car you are driving?

You know why I did…to be twenty one again **and** to know then what I know now !!!

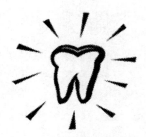

Nothing Beats a Toothache !!

Did you ever have a toothache?

Did you ever have a deadline to make?

Well, I am lucky enough to have both a toothache and a deadline to make today.

When you have a toothache, you do not know where to put yourself. My toothache was kind enough to wake me at 2:00 a.m. Now there are mornings when I wake at 2:00 a.m, accomplish the reason for which I woke at that ungodly hour, and then go back to sleep. With a toothache, you do not go back to sleep. You do not know where to put yourself. Should you walk around? Should you turn over in bed? Should you go into the bathroom, close the door and scream at the top of your lungs?

I chose none of the above options. I woke my husband. (kind, aren't I?) He is a retired periodontist so I thought I would share my dental woes with him at that hour. He's really a very kind man, and his advice was so professional.

"Take two Advil and we'll call a dentist in the morning."

In the morning? It *is* morning. I know he meant "at a civilized" time in the morning, but still… He, immediately, fell back to sleep and never even remembered my waking him while I was in the midst of a crisis. I, on the other hand, stared at the ceiling until daylight finally arrived.

I called my dentist, "calling in every favor" he ever owed my husband, and I was seen at the office at 7:30 a.m.

The dental assistant came in the operatory and took a couple of x-rays to see if any fracture or decay could be seen. I should be so lucky. Nothing could be seen on the x-ray.

The next step is the best: The dentist begins by *klopping* (banging) on the tooth and the adjacent teeth with the handle of the heaviest dental instrument in the tray. This is to determine which tooth is actually causing the problem. By the time he is finished banging on the teeth, the dentist actually believes you can identify which tooth is the problem tooth. All my teeth are screaming...after the *klopping*. My mouth feels like an army tramped through and set up an artillery base.

If I had an earache, the ENT physician would just *peek* in my ear, see the infection and prescribe an antibiotic. If I had broken my foot, the doctor would take an x-ray and put a cast on the broken foot. But the dentist comes in with every possible instrument, sets up shop, and starts banging on every tooth in your mouth. (In defense of my dentist and every dentist, there really is no other way for the dentist to determine the "problem" tooth.)

The results: The dentist discovered the *discomfort* is caused by an infected nerve canal. "*Discomfort*" (Don't you love it when they say "*discomfort*?" It's pain, Doc. It's pain.)

And I have this deadline today...

I know my articles usually have a Jewish slant...but I know no way to make this Jewish...except: My dentist is *Jewish* !! I have to go now. I need a root canal !!

I Didn't Steal Your Shopping Cart

Living in South Florida is so different from living in New York or Boston. In Florida, most people live in gated communities. Some communities remind me of Levittown where the homes resemble the plastic pieces from the well-known Monopoly game.

One day I was driving into our *"development,"* my mind was a million miles away as usual, and I drove into the wrong driveway. I pressed the garage door opener on my visor before I even entered the driveway, and as I approached the garage door, I almost drove straight through it.

The door never opened.

The garage door on the house next door was opening, however. My neighbor's house has different landscaping. We don't even have the same model home, but I was driving into his driveway. What is happening to me? Is the sun frying my brains down here?

I prayed no one saw me, but no such luck. My neighbor, standing across the street, was enjoying the show and laughing hysterically. When I sheepishly backed up to pull into my own driveway, I was tempted to run him over, but I let him live...this time.

Another incident that never happened to me before: I stole a man's shopping cart. I shop twice a week in The **Boys Farmers' Market** in Delray Beach. Shopping in the store is a novel unto itself.

You must maneuver up and down the aisles as if you were navigating an obstacle course. The obstacles that you must go around and avoid are the **People and their wagons**. The shoppers taste every piece of fruit offered them by the vendors as they walk along and push their carts. They walk slower than a snail moves. They examine every blemish on the peach, grape, or plum. The juice from the canteloupe they sampled is dripping down their chins. Yech !!

They leave their wagons in the middle of the aisle, stand beside it to taste and touch every piece of fruit on each side of them and expect the other shoppers to go around them. In frustration, I have left my wagon at the top of the aisle (out of the way), walked down the aisle, and chosen the product I want. I return to my wagon and go on to the next aisle and start all over again.

You wouldn't believe what I did one day. I took the wrong cart.

I did not realize this mistake until I heard an older man shrieking at the top of his lungs that his cart is gone with his groceries.

"***Someone took my cart***."

You'd think someone stole his life savings at gunpoint.

I looked down at my cart. Oh, sh#*#$. It's me. I have his cart. I was so embarrassed that I wanted to walk away from the wagon and begin shopping all over again. I knew there was going to be a "scene from hell" when I returned it to the man who was having a fit.

I was praying he wasn't carrying a weapon. Truthfully, he didn't look like he should even own a driver's license; never mind, a weapon. He made such a scene. No matter how many times I apologized to this man, you'd think I had taken his cart on purpose and was going to sell the goods on the "Black Market" as soon as I checked out of the store. I am so traumatized, to this day, that I food shop with one wrist handcuffed to the shopping cart.

The third incident is really an "accident" that can occur anywhere.

It happened to me in Boston as well as in Florida. In Florida, I shop at *Bed, Bath, and Beyond* in Boynton Beach. If you are not cashing out at the register, you tend to walk straight out of the store. There is only one problem with exiting that glass door. It is the *"enter"* door. You cannot believe the number of times I walked into that *"enter"* door.

In Boston I was walking through the glass corridor in Copley Place and also walked directly into the glass revolving door. The timing couldn't have been worse. It was three weeks before my son's wedding. It was the first time I had left the house in two-and-a-half months after undergoing "minor" cosmetic surgery. The final bandages had just been removed; it was my first outing, and **I walked into the glass revolving door** at the end of the Copley Place walkway.

I broke my nose.

Remember, it was three weeks to my son's wedding. I was catatonic thinking how great I'd look walking down the aisle on the arm of my husband with black and blue eyes staring out from bandages on my nose.

There is more glass in Florida than one could imagine. Buildings aren't made of concrete; I think they are made of glass. And all of it is tinted.

I believe that the Florida sun is frying my brains. I believe the majority of Florida residents are not only terrible drivers on the road but they are terrible drivers in the super markets with their shopping carts. Up north, I shop in *Stop & Shop*, and I have never stolen another person's shopping wagon. In

The Boys Farmer's Market in Delray, my picture is plastered on the Wanted Bulletin Board.

"Beware of dangerous shopper with wagon. She is five feet tall with lightly frosted blond hair. She is dangerous and known to steal others' shopping wagons."

That description could fit any woman living in Florida. No one is over five feet tall in Florida, and that is a "given."

Let me tell you, "Give a woman a shopping cart, and she becomes Mario Andretti in the super market."

It's the sun here. It's frying our brains.

I Refuse to Travel North in the Winter

We visited our relatives up north last week. We had an uneventful airplane trip, thank G-d, and we landed on a clear but cold day at Logan Airport in Boston. When we left Florida at noon, it was 79 degrees. When we landed in Boston at 3:00 p.m., it was 24 degrees, a regular heat wave.

In the ladies' room at Logan Airport, I put on my turtleneck jersey, wool sweater, winter coat, and heavy shoes to *shlep* through the mush on the sidewalks at the airport. I had been carrying all these items in a shopping bag through the terminals and stowing them in the overhead during the flight.

AND then, only twenty four hours after we arrived in Boston, G-d opened the heavens and sang, ***"Let it snow, let it snow, let it snow."*** And, it did…it snowed day after day after day.

Our neighbors were kind enough to lend us their father's car since the car was garaged at our house for the winter anyway. Their father was wintering in Florida. *Nu*, so we should know that *the car had no snow tires,* no all-season tires, only standard tires. We could drive it back and forth in the garage, but not out on the streets.

As of this writing, we have not been able to visit with our children and grandchildren because of the hazardous driving conditions. I don't care so much about my children. I know what they look like and sound like, but I do want to see my granddaughter. Her arms drape around my neck and hug me with so much trust and warmth and love, and she has a high pitched voice that melts my heart when she calls Papa and Grandma. She is two years old…and the love of my life.

I have no food in the house either. I have to borrow my friend's SUV to go to the market so we shouldn't starve. I wouldn't mind losing a few pounds, believe me, but starvation was not on my list of things to do this week. As I sit and write this e-mail, I can hear the snowplow driving by. I am trying not to think of the snow they are dumping in front of my driveway as they plow the street. Each time I hear the truck circle the block, I think "another six inches to shovel." I sometimes wonder if they bring the snow from other streets to dump in front of my driveway.

Did I mention Jerry and I both have bad backs and cannot shovel? We can only hire other people with snowplows and shovels and write checks to them to ease their lifestyle.

We open our checkbooks and say, *"Whatever you want to charge to plow our driveway, we are at your mercy. Fifty dollars, one hundred dollars, whatever you want, it's yours. In fact, here is a blank check. May G-d bless you and thank you."* I figure it's better than *our* attempting to shovel the snow and ending up in surgery for a disk problem.

Did I mention that the cable service to our home was temporarily disconnected for the season? Jerry searched the basement and found "rabbit ears" (an inside antenna) and attached it to the kitchen television. He knew he had to do something to alleviate my boredom and my screaming and my banging my head on the wall after watching the snowplow go around again. I was even tired of reading novels and writing e-mails. He managed to adjust the antenna so that we could, at least, access one television station.

Oh, sh*#, here comes the snowplow again. I'm going to run over to the window and wave to the driver...not with all five fingers, though.

If I thought I was lonely and missed being in Marblehead, Massachusetts, this past winter, I only have to reflect upon this week. I am aging. My blood is thinning, and Boca Raton, Florida, is the place to be. I love my northern friends, adore my family, and even miss them at times...but not enough to return here again in the winter...*unless* there's another grandchild in our future.

PS (Added months later)

There is another grandchild on the way...Guess when the due date is? JANUARY!!

Oh well, to return for that event is a Mitzvah!!

Oy, if it snows again like our last visit...Argh !!!!

Give Me a Hardwood Floor Any Day

Florida is definitely on the map now. Not only is it known for being the state to harbor the elderly and the Latino refugees, but Florida is infamous for its citizens' incapacity to punch the correct hole in a ballot in a Presidential voting election.

Officials from Palm Beach County hand counted ballots to decide who won the election for President of the United States in 2002. After counting them and spending our tax dollars, the courts found it was not an acceptable means to determine if each ballot was a valid vote.

I will not delve into this issue for fear of alienating half of my readers and for my inability to believe it really happened in this state and in this country.

Florida...Let's go on to lighter things in Florida...lighter, well? How about **whiter**?

I have a white tile floor throughout my entire house other than the bedrooms. I never had a white tile floor. I don't care if I ever have one again. I had rugs and a wood floor up north. I would "die" for that wood floor down here. I am a slave to this floor. If a drop of water spills anywhere, I don't have a prayer. Someone is going to step in it...just a little, and *schmootz* (mess) up the remaining tiles on the floor. After stepping in the water, the dirt from the bottom of your shoe becomes alive; it makes a life for itself on the bottom of your shoe and goes into every room with you. It leaves marks and footprints. Its enemy is vinegar and water and a swiffer.

I need an area rug in my living room. My "drekorator" told me to get a "Sizel." A Sizel is a straw rug. It is lovely, tropical, and looks great in a Florida home; however, it shows stains. Nothing can be dropped on it...not even water. Water actually stains a Sizel rug.

"No thanks, drekorator. I can not follow guests around at a party and pick up and wipe up whatever they drop on the floor." And, the *schmootz* must be removed within minutes from a Sizel rug. And, straw under your feet? Gee, that must be comfortable if you remove your shoes during the day and walk on the rug. Do you get splinters too?

What happened to "good old broadlooms and shag rugs?" Remember shag rugs? You vacuumed them, and the individual strands got caught in your vacuum. They were soft and comfy, though.

It rained today in Florida, and I had a furniture delivery. I just had my floors washed yesterday. The nice men brought the furniture in our house...in the pouring rain. Their footsteps look great on a white tile floor. I am going to get my vinegar and mop, and wash my floor for a change.

White tile floors, straw rugs, Yech !! Give me back my shag rugs and speckled linoleum !!

How to Run the Thermostat in Cold Weather in Florida

I never had problems adjusting the thermostat when I lived up north. When winter arrived, I set the thermostat to heat and set the temperature to 72 during the day and to 68 at night.

In Florida it's a whole different ballgame. Usually, the temperatures outside are in the upper 70's and 80's many days. (Hopefully…that's why we all moved down here). However, this past week the temperature in the evening and early mornings went down to the 30's and 40's so I set the thermostat to heat. I had to remind myself to *lower* the temperature setting so that my home didn't turn into a sauna.

The sun came up at 6 a.m. and the house began to warm up, so now I needed some air circulation. I had to remember to *raise* the temperature and put the setting to "cool." It was a marathon. I was running back and forth to my thermostat this past week because I could never remember whether it was on "*cool*" or "*heat*" and whether it was set for 77 degrees or 72 degrees.

I was grateful I only had one floor and one thermostat. Hopefully, the cold spell is over. I set the thermostat to "cool."

Now let's all enjoy the warmth of Florida and watch the weather channel to see how much snow they're getting up north…

I Think the Air-conditioning is Broken...

I awoke at 3:00 a.m. on a Friday morning and thought to myself, "*It's awfully hot in this bedroom.*" I knew it was not due to any extracurricular activity. He was snoring away.

I got out of bed to check the thermostat, stopped along the way for a "pit stop," since I was up and walking through the house anyway. At my age, if I'm up in the middle of the night and near a "way station," then I use that facility. I approached the thermostat. It was set at 77, and the fan was going. I could hear the whirring sound, but the thermostat was registering 79 degrees. Oy!!

I knew we were in for trouble. I could not worry alone at 3:00 a.m. so I woke Jerry to tell him something was wrong with the air conditioner. He was not a happy camper.

"*What do you want me to do at three in the morning? Call someone?*"

That sounded good to me...not practical, though.

He worried for a half of a second and fell asleep, snoring, and left me to look at the ceiling, *shvitzing* (sweating) and worrying by myself.

Now, for those of you who are not familiar with female midlife conditions, stress brings on hot flashes. So it was not only 79 degrees in the room at this point, but my body was experiencing a hot flash and reaching 179 degrees. I managed to fall asleep and woke at seven in the morning. Let me tell you, it was **HOT** in the bedroom. I flew to the thermostat and saw it was 82 degrees in the house, and it was only 7:00 a.m.

"Get up, Jerry, we're going to plotz here. They'll find our bodies in a few hours. Call the air-conditioning company."

"It's only 7 in the morning, and it's Saturday."

"Who cares what time it is or what day it is? Get up. The servicemen are working, believe me. There must be emergency service."

I am still wondering why I woke him. I could have made the phone call myself. I don't think I could stand to see him sleeping so comfortably while I was worrying for both of us.

Naturally, there was emergency service, and the serviceman appeared at our doorstep eight hours later. To make a long story short, we needed a new compressor and they had no idea how soon they would be able to replace it.

I shot the serviceman in the back as he turned to return to his truck. I kicked in the compressor with a sledgehammer, and Jerry was running down the street when I turned to him.

Do you know what it's like to live without air conditioning in Florida?

You don't even consider wearing make-up. You perspire and the make-up at the top of your forehead runs down your eyes, cheeks and nose, reaches your neck and drips on the collar of the shirt or sweater you are wearing. You now have a brown collar with your outfit. Your eye make-up is on your upper lip, and you look like you have a moustache. Your blush-on is under your chin. You could get a job with Barnum and Bailey circus.

If you try to towel dry your face wearing make-up, you smear the make-up. You look like you are wearing the "greasepaint of a clown, and there is no roar of the crowd." You may as well throw the towel away. I took a shower, dried off, and then needed to return to the shower again. I could have taken a shower every half hour on the hour.

At bedtime, I got into bed and my body stuck to the sheet. I turned over and the sheet went with me...and it's a fitted sheet too. We borrowed fans for the bedroom. Those are really good. They blow the **hot** air around the room.

I had to dress for temple for the holiday services. Putting on pantyhose could have won me an Olympic medal or thrown out my back. The hose stuck to my legs and to itself. When I walked, the inner thigh of my left leg wanted to attach itself to my right thigh. I looked like I was hopping. It was like wearing Velcro. I could hardly put on my clothes. Everything stuck to everything and weighed a ton. I felt like I was putting on a fur coat in the middle of summer.

And, the cooking for the Holiday...Oy!!!

I started cooking at 7:00 a.m. so the heat in the house would not be so intense. Because of the humidity, I swear the inside of my refrigerator was sweating as much as I was. You should only see what I was wearing when I was cooking...better you shouldn't see or even think about it!!!!

You know what was really amazing?

It was truly as hot as blazes in the bedroom when we went to sleep in the evening, and it took Jerry only *seconds,* and I mean *seconds*, to fall asleep. What gene does Man have to allow them that ability to fall asleep no matter what the conditions? His head doesn't even have to hit the pillow, and he is snoring! I, meanwhile, am lying in bed, contemplating the world's problems, tomorrow's activities, and everything from A to Z.

Well, we got the new compressor. The air conditioner is working, and all seems to be running smoothly. Now, what was that noise coming from the dryer?

Go West, Young Man

In Florida, the streets are laid out like a grid. There is north, south, east and west. When you drive to a destination, it is very easy to find your way. You drive either east toward the ocean or west toward the turnpike or north toward Orlando or south toward Miami.

If you need directions and ask a pedestrian, the individual instructs you to go north three miles, east two blocks, south 1/2 mile, badda, badda, boom...and you're there!!! They direct you to your destination by explaining that the location of the place in question is on the northwest corner. Great, no problem...if you know east from west. Once you move and live in Florida, you learn compass directions very fast. I don't know why. I couldn't figure it out in Geography 101, in the good ol' school days.

Now you go up north to Boston, New York, or any city or town in the northeast.

If you ask directions and the person tells you to go two blocks west, one mile south, and the place you are looking for is on the southeast corner, *you have taken more than one wrong turn. You are not in the northeast.* No one up north gives or takes directions by compass directions: north, south, east and west. Where is that in New England?

Directions are determined by landmarks: go past Haymarket Square and left at the library, or right at the John Hancock building and left at the next Mobil gas station, or right at the cinema. Now, everyone knows what everyone is talking about. G-d forbid, there's a detour or the gas station has been changed to a bank, you're back where you started. You don't know where you're going. You drive in circles. Asking directions in New England is actually laughable. Everyone knows where everything is; it's just that no one knows how to get there.

Finally, reaching your destination, you must try to find a parking place on the streets of Boston. There are as many parking lots in Boston as the fingers on one hand. Where do you park the car?

In Florida, every restaurant is in a shopping mall or located on a main street. There is plenty of parking spaces or there is always valet parking at the more trendy restaurants.

In New England, every restaurant is on a street with *"No Parking"* between the hours of 6:00 p.m. and 11:00 p.m., or resident parking only; or, on a street with meters that take a quarter for every fifteen minutes. You have to run out of the restaurant every hour to feed the meter four quarters. People at other tables see you leaving your table constantly and think you have a bladder problem and are running to the "john." You're running to feed the meters.

It is, indeed, a chore to drive anywhere in the city, any big city. The *Jackie Mason shtick* about the couple asking directions is so true. After asking directions of a passer-by, both people in the car immediately forget every direction he or she is given.

"I thought you were listening, and if you weren't listening, how do you know I'm going the wrong way?"

Everyone goes through the same thing, but no one talks about it. I do. That's why I'm the **BocaYente**.

Does the Bus Driver Know the Way?

Have you ever taken a day trip with your "community?"

Oh, boy!! I did, and that was a trip "to beat the band."

The best idea of the day was issuing a name tag with a specific color to indicate on which bus you were traveling. We could recognize the bus at a moment's notice and remember our name at the same time. The worst idea was hiring a bus driver who didn't know where he was going. I think he had just come over on a raft the day before.

At one point, passengers on the bus were using their cell phones to call their friends to give them directions so that they could relate the directions to the bus driver. He actually pulled the bus over on Route 95 *in the median strip* to communicate with the bus driver on the second bus.

Now this is not a smart place to park a bus for any given amount of time.

What should have been a 60 to 70-minute trip took two hours. We traveled the same roads in Miami Beach at least two times going in two different directions. I saw the east side of a street, and thirty minutes later I saw the west side of the same street. When we left the bus to tour at our first stop and put our feet on solid ground, we left articles of clothing on our seats. Naturally, when we returned to the bus, two ladies were sitting in our seats. They didn't like where they were sitting. They just picked up our clothes and put it in the back of the bus. My friend restrained me from opening the window and tossing out the ladies.

I knew I would return the gesture after our next stop which I did. I threw their clothes in the back seat when we returned after lunch. I just didn't know the next stop, which was ten minutes away, would take another hour.

We went from Miami Beach to Miami via one causeway, and realizing we should have remained in Miami Beach, returned to Miami Beach via another causeway…in noontime traffic. We were taking a trip along the intracoastal waterway on a bus instead of a boat since we crossed back and forth so many times in so many opposite directions. We actually went over one bridge in both directions.

People were grumbling, tempers were rising, and pleasantries among the passengers were becoming not so pleasant. Let me not forget to tell you about the bathroom in the bus…better yet, let me forget it !!

The *piece de resistance* was boarding the bus after the final stop to return back to our homes, and the bus didn't start. The battery was worn down.

Let me tell you, we were ready to push the bus to get back home or to kill the bus driver if he didn't get that motor to turn over. After G-d knows how many attempts, he managed to start the bus, and we headed north on Route 95 in five o'clock rush-hour traffic. I could have walked faster than the bus moved.

A six-hour day trip turned into a nine-hour marathon. The next trip is in March…guess who is ***not*** going to be on it?

Snowbirds Fly South <u>after</u> Yontif (holiday)

Seasons seem to fly by faster with every passing year; and soon after the Jewish New Year, *Rosh Hashanah*, Papas and Grandmas return to Florida, the land of sunshine and "no snow."

Years ago, when the state, Florida, was mentioned, people visualized little old gray-haired grandparents *shlepping* with the aid of canes and walkers to board airline flights to escape the northeast winters. Today, the Papas and Grandmas are vibrant, youthful middle-aged adults. They no longer have gray hair or "vintage blue." Grandma's hair is blonde or brunette. Grandparents are still *shlepping,* but they're *shlepping* golf clubs and tennis rackets, mah jong and canasta cards, and lap-top computers.

These "wandering Jews" are called **Snowbirds**. They live in Florida in the winter and in the northeast in the summer. Some snowbirds travel by air, some snowbirds rest their wings and drive their own automobile; and some snowbirds take the Amtrak autotrain and need drive only a few hundred miles.

It's an interesting experience to drive in a closed compartment with your spouse for days on end. It's no different from the trips my husband and I took years ago when our boys were younger.

We leave early in the morning to get the jump on the commuter traffic. We stop every two hours…for the same reason the kids did, and we must stretch our backs and walk around at each rest stop. If we don't "loosen our vertebra," we will be as stiff as boards and will need those canes and walkers.

We travel with food to *nosh* (snack) on, and we always travel with water. Perhaps that is the reason we have to stop at rest stops so frequently. We have maps galore, a map for each state. We have trip-ticks from Triple A with our route highlighted in red. We have books on tape to listen to and pillows to rest our *keppies (heads)*.

We talk to each other during the trip which is a plus. You'd think we would run out of conversation during the 1600 miles, but we find what to talk about. Our kids thought we would kill each other during these long automobile trips, but we haven't yet. We have been tempted, but so far, so good.

We call ahead to a reputable hotel, calculate our ETA (estimated time of arrival) and book a room for the night. We stay on the first floor so we don't have to drag our overnight bag up a flight of stairs, and we park our car in front of the room so I can jump up 300 times during the night to see if the car and its belongings are still there. I haven't decided what I would do if I didn't see the car. Faint? Wake my husband and the other travelers with a primordial scream? Or plan when and where I can replenish my wardrobe?

You know you've left New England and traveled more than halfway to Florida when the heat begins to permeate the interior of the car. Jeans are changed for shorts at a rest stop, and the northeastern part of the United States is now in the rear-view mirror.

Snowbirds Fly North for Passover

How does a Jewish snowbird know when to *leave* Florida and return north to Boston, New York, or any hometown?

They know because of *Passover*. If Passover were ever deleted from the calendar, the Jews would be like the Lost Tribes of Israel. They would be wandering the streets of Delray Beach, Boca Raton, and Boynton Beach, waiting for the trumpets to sound, to inform them that it's O.K. to pack and to go back north for the summer. Winter is over.

The Snowbirds want to be with their family for Passover, and the family usually live in the northeast,

When Passover arrives, the airlines raise their prices, the airports become crowded, the highways become jammed with auto transports heading east, and UPS begins their pony express delivery from south to north.

Florida homes are temporarily closed with the air conditioner set on higher levels. Some do not even use their air conditioner at all during the winter months. They use the excuse, "*I like the fresh air*," as perspiration drips down their forehead.

Spring in Boston and New York is heralded by the arrival of the Floridian Jews. Now the north comes to life. Crates of oranges stop arriving from the south. Automatic timers are disconnected from the northern residences, and electric lights are run manually. Tanned faces become intertwined with pale faces at the deli counter, at neighborhood temples, and at local hairdressing salons.

"You look wonderful," everyone says, *"so tanned."*

What they mean is, *"You look wrinkled from the ravages of the sun."*

As Passover marks the departure from Florida, so does Rosh Hashanah and Yom Kippur mark the return to Florida. What would we do without a Jewish calendar?

We would be pacing in the house wondering, "Do we pack today or tomorrow? Yesterday? Should we have packed yesterday? When do we leave for Florida? Oy!! Hymie, get the Jewish calendar."

Western Wall

Don't Run...Walk

We visited the Holy land. We planned for months to visit this Jewish nation.

Israel is a land of desert and farmland; and, in Tel Aviv, it is a land of cobblestones. One cobblestone had my husband's name on it. He slipped and fell and broke his foot on the third day of touring Israel. He was running, and he fractured his metatarsal. I actually heard the bone snap.

"No, this couldn't happen here in Israel. We just began our tour of the country with our friends. We planned this trip for two years." I said to myself.

I wanted to ignore this man lying on the sidewalk and continue walking, but this piteous voice was calling, *"Phyllis, help me. I think I broke my foot."*

"Jerry, you couldn't have. Try walking on it."

He tried. He cried. He screamed. It was definitely broken.

Our guide drove us to the hospital in Tel Aviv which was comparable to visiting a Children's Zoo on a weekend. Not only did they not speak English, they did not speak in a normal tone. They shouted. The noise level was off the decibel chart, and everyone had cigarettes dangling from their lips in this supposedly sterile hospital.

We managed to see a doctor who was curt, arrogant and had the heart of the Tin Man from *The Wizard of Oz*. He spoke only Hebrew, only to our guide, and we thought we were invisible. What was interesting was upon our leaving the examining room, he said to Jerry (in excellent English), *"Keep your foot up for three days to relieve the swelling and then go to a hospital in Jerusalem for a plaster cast."*

We looked at each other. The *stinker* spoke English.

There were six of us in our private touring group. The two other couples were dear friends who wanted to put Jerry out of his misery. *They shoot horses, don't they*? However, we found a purpose for Jerry. While we toured, he could sit in the car and guard our valuables.

Three days later we arrived in Jerusalem. We went to *Shaare Zedek Hospital*. It was closed. Did you ever hear of a hospital being closed to emergencies? We had to purchase a newspaper which listed the hospitals open for emergencies on that given day. We went to the Hadassah Hospital. Everyone raves about it so we thought it would be wonderful. Right? Wrong!!

The doctors said it was not an emergency. It happened three days ago. They would not look at his foot. The doctors and the guide were now screaming at one another. We were shown to the exit.

Where do we go now? In Israel socialized medicine is prevalent and no private doctors are available so we had to go to a Public Health Center. A Public Health Center is comparable to the old Boston City outpatient/emergency room on a Saturday night or Bellevue Hospital in New York. We were seen by a technician but Jerry was not treated by him at that time. We were to come early in the morning on the next day, and a technician or physician would cast his foot up to his knee.

Our guide could not accompany us on the next day but I felt I would be able to handle the situation.

Oh, my G-d, you should have seen what it was like at eight in the morning. We walked in, and there must have been five different lines with thirty people in each line waiting for treatment…and naturally, everyone was shouting.

I looked at Jerry who really was in pain and had been a great sport about this whole fiasco.

"Sit down on the bench. I'm taking over. I have had it." I said with total disgust for people who acted like animals, and for a country that enabled this state of confusion called socialized medicine.

I dragged a chair into this mob of people, stood on it and screamed louder than I had ever screamed at my kids' little league games, *"Does anyone speak English?"*

You could hear a pin drop…but only for a second. A woman approached me, pointed to Jerry, and I nodded, yes. I was tempted to nod no. She led me to the head of a line, knocking down three old ladies, two Arabs, four children and a partridge in a pear tree.

I thanked her over and over, turned to the nurse who was on the other side of the desk and in broken English explained the situation. I spoke English as if Greek were my native tongue, and I was shouting as if she would understand better.

"Leg broken. Swelling gone. Need cast," gesturing and pointing with both hands, and I'm a speech therapist in the United States, yet.

They led me to an examining room after I explained it was my husband, not me, who had the broken metatarsal. The doctor entered. He said nothing and began setting the cast.

He asked, *"Are you a Jewish man?"*

"Yes," My husband answered with trepidation. Why was he asking this question?

The doctor looked at Jerry, *"I could guess because of your long nose."*

The cast dried within the hour and as we were ready to leave, I asked how much we owed him.

"Go and enjoy Israel," were his words to us. When I heard his words, I became a dishrag and cried non-stop, allowing three days of frustration and aggravation flow down my cheeks in the form of tears. We shook hands. I would have kissed his feet at that point. We took a cab back to the hotel and Jerry slept for the remainder of the day. Touring for him was tortuous and exhausting, but he went everywhere, at a slower pace than the others; but he persevered and traveled with us wherever he could maneuver a cast and crutch. He even made it to the top of the Masada.

I became the *shleppe*r. I *shlepped* the camera, the camera bag, the backpack with the sweaters in it, his medicines, water. You name it, I had it. Originally, Jerry was to be the chief photographer since photography was one of his favorite hobbies. He did not bring his automatic camera. He brought the camera that had to have 300 adjustments made before snapping the photo. I now became the *Designated Photographer* and after a few lessons I became really good. Move over, Annie Leibowitz.

When we first arrived in Israel, I saw a most beautiful diamond mezuzah neckpiece. I couldn't resist it, but I did feel guilty about spending the money. After twelve days of *shlepping* equipment and luggage and pushing Jerry in wheelchairs through museums and airports, I was already looking for matching earrings.

Did we enjoy the trip? We loved the country. We were disgusted with the medical treatment, and traveling for Jerry was tortuous at times. We can't laugh at this situation yet, and I really don't think we ever will.

Would we do it again? In a minute…if Jerry watched where he was walking.

"Whose Sock is This Anyway?"

Have you ever taken a vacation with five other couples...everyone sleeping under one roof? We did this past summer. Our friends from Florida own a house on Cape Cod and invited four other couples and us to stay over for one week.

Each day began with a chorus of toilet flushing during the early morning hours. Beginning at two in the morning, a toilet flushed every half hour on the hour. After all, we're not kids anymore. Two couples shared one bathroom. We were to leave the door open after we used the facilities so that anyone going in the middle of the night would know it was unoccupied. The bathrooms were the busiest rooms in the house. At one point during the night, the three toilets flushed at once, and it sounded like Niagara Falls.

We met downstairs around eight in the morning, and everyone sat around the kitchen table with juice and their pills. We all compared the virtues of our pills with our neighbor's pills. We had a pill for high blood pressure, thyroid imbalance, osteoporosis, mild diabetes, high cholesterol, you name it.

Many hilarious incidents occurred during that week. For instance, at dinner, one evening, our hostess opened three bags of shrimp to be grilled. She made one small error. She thought each bag held one pound of shrimp (40 shrimp). Well, each bag held two pounds of shrimp. Multiply that by three bags of shrimp, and we grilled 240 shrimp for dinner...for ten people. We almost *bleched* by the time we finished dinner.

One day we took a car trip to Provincetown. The women always traveled in one car, and the men traveled in another car. Imagine five women talking at once; we got so *fahrmished* (mixed-up) we drove around a rotary twice until we found the correct cutoff; one person was yelling to go one way, another was yelling to go another. It was a challenge to be the driver in the womens' car. Meanwhile, the men in the front car kept calling us on the cell phone to make sure we were heading in the right direction.

I could tell you story after story but I will tell you one incident that will remain in our minds forever. Three women, Charlotte, Marilyn, and Myrna, decided to do laundry...their underwear and their husbands' underwear. And, these geniuses washed their underwear ***together.***

I want you to imagine approximately 30 pairs of socks, bras, men's jockey underwear, boxer shorts and assorted lingerie piled onto one bed, *and* each woman had to figure out what belonged to whom.

The men became hysterical. "*I am not going to wear these pants. What if they're not mine? I can't think about that possibility. It's too personal. What if they're Carl's pants? They'll strangle my you-know-what.*"

They eventually sorted the underclothes; G-d knows who is wearing whose...but what an evening of laughter...what a week of laughter...what a wonderful time. The day ended in the wee hours of the morning after numerous hilarious games of Mexican train cars (don't play with Abe...you could pass away until he takes his turn). Every evening we all fell into our beds, and the lullabye of the evening was *A Chorus of Snoring.* Five men snoring at one time under one roof.

Would we do it again? In a minute!! Did you hear that, Myrna and Carl? We're all available, G-d willing, next summer.

Do Jewish Girls Really Camp Out?

I have been accused of being a JAP because I don't like "roughing it."

Well, let me tell you about roughing it since I did that in my earlier days when my children were younger…and yes, I still can remember that "togetherness vacation."

It began by packing a car with necessities such as food and blankets, sleeping bags, matches to start a fire, tents (that are easy to assemble). Right…like there is such a thing!!! Games and activities to keep the little children occupied; cooking utensils, toilet paper, *Kleenex*, paper towels, etc. You are exhausted before you back your car out of the driveway, and you usually end up packing on the hottest day of the year.

The three-hour ride is always a pleasure with the children in the back seat.

"His leg touched me. He's staring at me. He's not staring at me. He's making faces at me. I don't like this music. Change the radio station."

"Oh my G-d, this is going to be a fun trip." I can tell already.

The bathroom stops are more frequent than the stops at the highway toll booths…and when you can't find a bathroom, they refuse to go into the woods alongside the road. Yet these same children are going to live and camp in the woods for days.

Assembling the tent is a feat no Jewish girl should attempt, and you must be young to accomplish this and *meshugina,* to even attempt it.

The bathrooms in the campground have an odor unto themselves. You beg the kids not to go to the bathroom until next week. You'll give them a bonus in their allowance, anything. Please don't make Mommy and Daddy go with you. The smell will permeate your nostrils for years. And for certain, the kids usually have to go at night when you must walk around the woods with a flashlight to find the outhouses...and pray to G-d not to happen upon an animal or a reptile that slithers along the ground.

What do you do at a campground? You hike through poison ivy, climb rocks and cut your knees, wave to other suffering mothers and fathers (no one you recognize, believe me), and swim in the lake, UNTIL it starts to rain.

At home when it rains, the children go into another room and play. In a tent, the children are in the <u>same</u> space, in the <u>same</u> tent with you. What togetherness. And, where is Dad at this point? He's sitting in the car crying!! So, roughing it? Feh!!

A hotel with a supervised children's activity center sounds good. And, what sounds even better? Leave the darlings at home with their grandparents or a sitter and enjoy a well-deserved vacation with or without spouse.

If I don't enjoy roughing it and I like clean sheets under my body at night; and, if I like having someone serving me dinner at a lovely restaurant and listening to the sound of the waves just a short distance away makes me a JAP, then I'm a JAP. At least, I'm not a phony who ***claims*** they prefer showering in the woods rather than relaxing at a pool or beach on a tropical island.

Tell me the truth, don't you prefer a hotel with indoor plumbing?

Time to Move to Florida...
Time to Sell our House up North....

"Good-bye, 9 Fieldbrook Road, Marblehead," and I say it with a heavy heart. We finished packing 27 years of "stuff," and now we must leave this house forever.

Jerry and I raised two wonderful sons in this home, watched them grow and then watched them leave to travel their own paths and make their own way in life.

At this time, one son lives in Miami, Florida, and the other lives in Ashland, Massachusetts. They, too, have their many memories at 9 Fieldbrook Road.

Brad, my older son, remembers his TV being in the front hall more than in his bedroom. That was his punishment for doing something wrong (missing Hebrew school, hitting his brother, etc.).

Michael, my younger son, remembers his bedroom door always closed because he was such a "slob" that I couldn't look in his room when I passed by; and besides, his music was deafening and he listened to "hard rock." Brad's bedroom, on the other hand, was immaculate.

Our backyard, 27 years ago, had a wooden gym and swing set on the grass for the kids to play on. Today, years later, the swing set is gone, and the yard is beautifully groomed with plants and flowers and shrubs.

Our study was a porch years ago. Today it is a computer/study room. Twenty-seven years ago there was a piano in the basement for the boys to practice their piano lessons. Today the basement looks like a furniture storehouse, and the piano is gone.

Brad's bedroom, today, has a "pac n play" for the grandchildren and a bed for an overnight guest.

We had wonderful parties at 9 Fieldbrook Road, and we sat shiva (mourning) here also. In the 27 years we lived here, we both lost our parents, but gained two beautiful grandchildren, and another on the way...in January, 2001, G-d willing.

If I could speak to this house I would say,

"Thank you for caring for us for the past 27 years. We have known joy, and we have known sorrow within these walls, but thank G-d, the joy has outweighed the sorrow. We have huddled by your fireplace when snow was falling, and we have rested during the hot summer days in the comfort of central air conditioning. We had to paint you many times and you had a facelift (me too); but, you always remained constant and reliable. We may have updated your bedrooms to a guest room and a music room, but I still refer to them as Brad's room and Michael's room. I look in the rooms and remember the boys that are now men. You watched us all grow; and, as our children left you to go on to their next stage in life, so must Jerry and I leave you to go on to our next stage in life...and thank G-d, it's not to the Jewish Rehabilitation Center at this point. It's on to Florida, to another way of living and doing what we want to do today and tomorrow, although not within your walls.

So, 9 Fieldbrook Road, Thank you...and good-bye. Thank you for all the memories and may you take care of the new people who will be living here. I hope they will love you as I do."

Downsizing

I discovered a way to "downsize." It's a sneaky plan but it works if you do it casually.

For example, one day I baked some cookies and put them on a piece of my finest china. I brought the platter with the cookies to the children. They loved the cookies, and they thought the cookies looked great on the platter. I told the kids I loved them so much the platter was theirs to keep.

"No, no, Mom. Thanks anyway. We don't need it."

"O.K., I told them. I'll pick it up next time I visit."

Next time I visited I brought them a cake. I put the cake on another beautiful platter and managed to forget to take that platter home as well.

Got the picture? Every time I visited I brought them another piece of the china until finally, I asked if they would like the dining room set to match.

They thought we were dying since we were giving away all our dishes and furniture. We weren't dying; we were *downsizing*. We were moving to Florida.

I wanted to buy "all new." A new start, in a new place, with new furnishings.

You'd think the children would want to take all of our valuables. But guess what? They're not valuable to the children. They only have sentimental value to us. What I thought was beautiful: white china dishes with the gold rim, the kids think is old-fashioned.

What about all the photographs? You must convince your children to be the "Keeper of the Memories."

There are no basements in Florida so you ask if you can store your winter clothes in their basement. Inside the boxes of winter clothing, hide all the loose photographs and albums. It's the children's turn to keep the photographs anyway. Of course, no one knows who anyone is in the pictures. Those who could identify those in the photos passed away years ago.

What do I do with all the *yarmulkes* from Bar Mitzvahs we attended? What about my four mezuzahs, the many baking dishes and pots and pans? I was buying all new kitchen accessories; I didn't need them down in Florida.

And, the hardest part was having my children take what was "***theirs***."

"*It's your stuff, kids. It's not my karate uniform or baseball trophy. Time to store your own stuff. They're your memories.*"

We chose not to have a yard sale since we had one the previous year, and I did not think I could survive another one. One yard sale in a lifetime is enough.

Remember *stuff* does not make memories. Stuff *triggers* memories.

Memories are warm cozy thoughts, usually about special people; and, you carry people in your heart.

Don't worry: Your memories are not thrown away with your *stuff.*

Take Me, I'm Free

What a summer !! We spent the summer packing. Actually, *I* did the majority of the packing since my husband ruptured a disc and required back surgery three days after arriving in New England. His timing was impeccable, wouldn't you say?

In October, 2000, we moved into Cascade Lakes in Boynton Beach, Florida. We loved every single day of Floridian lifestyle and decided to sell our home up north the following summer. Why own and maintain two properties? We could rent up north in the summers and even do a little traveling while we could still walk without the aid of walkers.

We decorated our home in Florida over the winter with new furniture and appliances like a bride and groom and bought new *stuff*.

Winter is over, however, and we are back in New England and we must empty an entire home filled with eight rooms of furniture and *stuff*. Everything has to go.

Where do you begin? First, you inform the children whom you believe will line up and take everything.

"No thanks, Mom, it's not my taste. I'll take the computer stuff though, Dad. Maybe, I'll take the dining room set but I don't want you to put the photograph albums in the drawers so that I become the keeper of the photos and mementos."

They **must** take the albums and photographs. In Florida the photographs will ruin in the hot attic, and where is a basement when you need one? You can't throw those pictures out. Those photograph albums are our family tree even if we don't recognize one face. I hid them in the boxes that my son is storing for us in his attic. Someday he's going to "kill me" when he finds them, but he will have a smile on his face. He'll probably spend hours looking at them, explaining to his children who's who, if he even knows. I wrote a name and date on the back. Even if he gets a little angry, I have a feeling I'll be long gone from this world. So big deal !!

But the little things that must be given away: kitchenware, *tchotchkees,* telephones, ironing board, an iron, odds and ends. The list goes on and on. We did sell a lot of things by advertising in the newspaper, and we did not have a yard sale since we had one last year. There was no way on earth I could go through another yard sale. One yard sale in a lifetime is enough.

Trash collection day is every Tuesday where we lived. Late Monday afternoon I put out "stuff" with a sign that said in big, bold letters: ***Take me, I'm Free.*** I put out my ironing board and displayed all kinds of pots and pans. My husband displayed his old tools and fishing rods and "stuff" that he had saved since his college days. I put out books and even furniture that Salvation Army wouldn't pick-up.

During the day, cars drove by our home, checking out the "stuff." They drove slowly, but not one car stopped.

During the middle of the night, however, when it was quite dark, it was a different story. Cars were not driving by slowly. They were lining up in front of our home to take their selection of free "stuff." People who were too embarrassed to take anything during the daylight were taking everything during the evening hours. We did this every single week until moving day. People were waiting for our *trash.* We were famous in our area. Nothing was left.

That is how you get rid of "stuff." "Take me, I'm free."

In the year 2001 we returned to Marblehead, Massachusetts for the summer. We sold our house in Marblehead, and we were renting someone else's home.

The Location was "To Die For"... the Interior of the House, Oy !

The BocaYente and her husband, Jerry, are in Marblehead, Massachusetts, for the summer. We just arrived. We unpacked most of the clothes from the car and we were exhausted from driving the 1600 miles.

By eleven o'clock in the evening, we couldn't put another stitch of *wrinkled* clothing away or empty another box or bag.

"Let's just go to sleep already, Phyllis."

We got into bed and all of a sudden a fly is buzzing around my head. It is the size of a quarter and doing somersaults and kami-kaze maneuvers you wouldn't believe possible.

"Jerry, kill it."

"What would you like me to kill it with?"

"Spray it."

"With what, Phyllis?"

"Bug spray, what do you think?"

"O.K., where is it?"

"Why don't you look downstairs in the hall closet and under the kitchen sink, and I'll look around up here in the closets and bathroom?"

Of course, we couldn't find any bug spray.

"I'll put the light on in the bathroom, and it will fly in there for the night, Phyllis."

"Oh, that's good. If the fly's buzzing doesn't keep me up, the light's reflection will."

"I'm going to spray it with hair spray, Jerry."

Picture me running around chasing a fly with hair spray. The mist from it was falling onto my head, and now not a hair was out of place, nor will it be for another week, I'm sure.

"Jerry? G-d almighty, are you sleeping? How can you sleep with the fly in here?"

"I am having no trouble sleeping with the fly buzzing around. I am having trouble sleeping with you chasing a flying insect and spraying it with hair spray."

He was snoring, and I am chasing a fly with $12 hair spray, and the fly was going just as strong; actually, he was moving stronger than I was by this time. And, you-know-who is snoring away. Finally, I could stand it no longer and decided I was going to use strong ammunition.

I sprayed it with <u>Spray Starch</u>…and I got it! The wings couldn't move. The fly was *plotzing*. He flew out of the room and "passed away."

I crawled into bed next to the Snorer, and all night wondered "where did the fly finally die?" I still haven't found him, but I'm checking every nook and cranny in this place.

HOLIDAYS

Which Menorah Should We Use This Year?

There are many "givens" that accompany a holiday.

When you think of Chanukah, or Hanakah, or however you spell it, you think of dreidles that spin, and potato latkes that are delicious, fattening, and unhealthy to eat. You think of presents: toys for the younger children, *gelt* for the teenagers, and clothes for the adults in the family.

Whether the clothes are ever worn by the adults is a mystery. Have you ever seen your son wear a shirt you bought him? Better to give a gift certificate and let him choose his own present.

At Chanukah you think of menorah candles and the ***four*** menorahs you have stored in the buffet in the dining room. Why do we own more than one menorah? Which one should we use this year? The modern one? The classic one? The sterling one? The one from Israel?

And, which way do we light the candles? From right to left, left to right? Do we stand in front of the menorah? Behind? What color candles should we use tonight?

This year Chanukah is the day after Thanksgiving. What does Thanksgiving remind us of? Turkey and stuffing, and everyone sitting around a table eating and talking, not exactly in that order.

Thanksgiving also reminds me of *traffic*. Everyone is traveling on Wednesday to be "home" for Thanksgiving on

Thursday. In our younger years when my husband and I returned from Philadelphia, driving on a Wednesday night after my husband's classes, I remember sitting in the car, backed up for miles on the New Jersey Turnpike. The trip would take us a minimum of eight hours. We would arrive at my parents' home after midnight, and the first thing out of my mother's mouth would be, *"So where's your lipstick? You're not wearing any."*

I remember calling Rt. 95 in Boston by its original name, Rt. 128; and, I remember it as a parking lot rather than a highway. It still is a parking lot, especially at commuter time.

However, what stands out most in my mind about past Thanksgivings: The "airport runs" to pick up the kids from college at Logan airport. No one child ever arrived at the same time. More than one trip to the airport during the week of Thanksgiving was without question a definite. What a nightmare that was, and now it is a Horror Show!!

Where's the ramp to the airport entrance this week? Is it on the right or the left of Rt. 1A? Are the arrival gates still on the ground floor or do we have to drive up the ramp? Is Delta still in the same terminal? Will the kids have their luggage or is their suitcase on the way to Minneapolis?

Those were the years when you had to go to the airport for the children, one by one, and the grandparents, who decided to descend on us for the holidays.

But this year will be different. We are the ones who will be flying in for the holidays this year. For the first time, we will be on the other end of the pickup. Payback time !

Or is it? We're thinking of calling a car service. We wouldn't want to inconvenience anybody.

Hint, hint…

Happy Thanksgiving and Happy *Chanukah* or *Hanukah* or *Hanakkah*!!!!!!!!

Is It Early or Late This Year?

Summer will soon be over, and fall will be at our doorstep. Leaves will fall from the trees, heavier sweaters will be retrieved from the closet, and shorts and t-shirts will be stored away for the next year.

Rosh Hashanah is approaching. Is it early or late this year?

That should be the 5th question asked at the Passover Sedar. Why do we really need to know?

I suppose we should plan on whom will be home for the holidays. Will the kids be in public school and will we have to take them out for those days? Then they'll have homework to make up and *kvetch* about missing certain classes. Will the older ones come home from college or will they not want to make the trip back to the north shore?

Jews prepare for the holiday in many different ways. Some buy new clothes to wear to Temple. G-d forbid, they should be seen in an outfit from last year. Would other people really remember? *I* don't remember what I wore last year. Did I wear summer clothes or winter clothes? Was it warm or cool? Actually, I don't even remember what I wore yesterday.

Some Jews prepare by cooking and freezing the fourteen or more courses for the holiday dinner. This holiday is a time when families get together to share a meal, usually following temple services. No little league games to *shlep* the kids to, no errands to run, no one rushing to work. How many times does a family get to enjoy a meal together? Not enough times.

Other Jews prepare by rehearsing their spoken *"aliyah"* that is delegated to them by the "Powers" of the temple. These "Powers" are chosen individuals who usually give of themselves either physically or monetarily to the workings of the temple. Both of these groups of congregants are necessary to run a temple. Running a temple is a business.

At my home, seventeen of us sit down to eat the holiday dinner...unless someone has a friend who has no place to go and, *nu*...he or she also comes to my home. So we squeeze in at the table. No one should be alone at the holidays. Everyone invited pitches in by cooking and bringing one dish, clearing the dishes after dinner, and watching their own children. After dinner when everyone is stuffed, we sit around and reminisce, talk, tell stories and jokes and enjoy each other's company without rushing for a change.

It's the beginning of a New Year. For some people, it is exciting. Maybe a new child is expected or another child is going away to college or another is engaged to be married. Mitzvahs ahead...For others, it may be an anxious time in their lives. They fear the year ahead may be a rough one, due to illness or business reversals, family upheavals or changes, or other avenues they never dreamed of traveling.

Why does it always seem that a few loved ones passed away during the previous year and that one person from the dinner table is missing with each holiday? On the other hand, the person missing has made space for a younger one to have a place at the table. One goes and one comes.

Do you read the obituary column? I always know when Rosh Hashanah is approaching by the obituary column. That's the truth. I say to my husband, *"There's more Jewish names near the onset of the holidays than at any other time of the year."*

It's like G-d said, *"You weren't written in the Book of Life for the following year, and I forgot to take you. You must come with me now before the New Year begins."*

Where is time going? Why is it harder to get up every morning than the morning before? Why is it harder to prepare for company than it was the year before? Why do I see extra gray hairs that weren't there yesterday? Why do some days have speed bumps in them that are harder to cross than in previous years when I was younger and had the stamina?

The question is moot. It's the beginning of a New Year. With every year we age. We hope we age with health and prosperity and with peace in our hearts, but we do hope we age.

I reflect on this forthcoming holiday with hope and love in my heart for my family and friends. I wish for them what I would wish for my loved ones and myself.

I wish for all…A Very Happy, Healthy New Year

L' Shanah Tovah

Another Look at the Holiday

Yontif (holiday referring to Rosh Hashanah) is almost here. It is a time for joy, for cooking, for meditation, and a time for shopping. We must buy new clothes for the holiday. We don't want to be seen in last year's outfit. Why everyone surely remembers what we wore last year. After all, they looked us over from head to toe.

Remember when we had to enter the temple and as we walked to our seat, we could feel everyone's eyes on us. We prayed we didn't have a run in our stocking or our dress wasn't stuck in the back of our underpants. We walked through those sanctuary doors and the eyes of G-d were not only upon us, but the eyes of the members.

We always say, *"Happy New Year"* to our friends as we walk to our seats (which had better be the same seats as last year or they'll hear from us), smile at other members who sit near us; and we know we are being "checked out."

"Hmm, she put a little weight on since last year" or *"she certainly has more lines in her face this year"* or *"wonder where her husband is."*

And when the children enter the sanctuary... They are adorable and everyone *oohs* and *aahs* and the children are dressed to a "T." The parents enter as proud as peacocks holding their children within their arms...children, who were screaming no more than five minutes ago. They were told by their parents, in those five minutes, about being quiet in temple or *"they'll be sorry,"* and they had better behave nicely like the Goldberg children.

The teens enter sporadically. They do not want to be there. They don't want to wear a jacket and tie. They haven't worn one since their Bar Mitzvah. They squirm in their seats, mumble under their breath, and they look at the clock and leave as fast as their parents will allow.

When my children were younger they were under the same orders as the children today. *"Don't open your mouth unless it's an emergency, and here's a piece of candy. Suck this and try to be quiet."* I sat them next to my husband so they could play with the fringes on his tallis.

My husband passed out one year when we were standing for the Kol Nidre service. Actually, **he fell asleep standing,** honest to G-d. He started to fall forward, and my older son and I had to grab him or there would have been a domino effect on everyone standing. Have to admit, we laughed like "heck." (quietly).

My kids didn't have to sit that long in our temple because we had to *shlep* over to the next town to visit my parents who went to *Shul* (orthodox temple). We had to visit my parents or it would be a *shunder* (shame) that their children and grandchildren were the only ones who didn't visit their parents in *Shul* at the holidays. Right!! I wonder who thought up that line. I use it now on my adult children and their children. *Thanks, Mom and Dad, it works.* It's called **guilt.**

Yontif is a holiday filled with happy and sad feelings. You know you should stay longer in temple to pray, but hope that G-d will understand that you have to get home to prepare the food for the onslaught of the family in a couple of hours…and you hope he will ***Please Inscribe your Family's Name in the Book of Life for another Year.***

Good *Yontif*, folks……

It's an Eating Marathon

The holidays are almost here, and I will probably gain ten pounds.

Rosh Hashanah is one of the highest Jewish holidays, but it is also the beginning of the J*ewish Eating Marathon.* The event is held in cities and suburbs throughout the world. It can be compared to the Italian Festival in Boston's North end.

The Italian people in the North End have a parade and have food vendors all over the streets. We have our own parade in our temples, and our vendors are the hosts at family dinners.

The temple parade begins by our walking down the center aisle, dressed "in our finest." We are called for an *aliyah* (honor). We stop at every row and shake hands with the lucky person sitting on the aisle seat. Sometime we even get a kiss on the cheek. We acknowledge people we only see from one year to another. We don't even remember the names of those kissing us. It takes thirty minutes to return to the seat. Then the hand shaking begins all over again. Those sitting beside you shake your hand, those sitting behind you, those sitting in front of you. It goes on and on; instant bursitis. I once turned to my husband and kissed him. I forgot he walked beside me for the aliyah.

My nieces and their families sit behind us at temple. I can hear everything they are saying, and they don't stop talking. I usually ask them who's this one parading down the aisle, who's that one with the big hat? I want to know who's in the parade too. The odds are favorable that one of my nieces will know. I know the "older generation," and they know the younger generation."

Following temple services, everyone heads for the home where dinner will be served and where the food vendors have been cooking for days. Then the eating orgy begins.

In our family we head for my sister's home since my husband and I no longer have a permanent residence on the north shore. We start with three hors d'oeuvres, continue on to soup and then to gefilte fish. The two choices of a main course are served with five different side dishes. Course after course of food is served. Desserts are the "killer" but we manage to "sample" each one of them. G-d forbid, we should pass up tasting a dessert.

Following Rosh Hashanah, we have eight days to rest and to eat normally. We refrain from eating on Yom Kippur to do a little praying; and at sunset, we begin eating all over again. Yom Kippur is not a fast day; it's a resting day till we start eating again.

At the Italian festival in Boston, it's noisy in the streets. At our festival, it's noisy in the homes…with the children *kvitching and kvetching;* and, so many of them. Are they all ours or did they come off the street?

The families grow larger with every passing year. Who's complaining? That is the best part of life.

As far as the eating marathon is concerned, what would Rosh Hashanah be without gefilte fish and horseradish to clear the sinuses, chicken soup with the "soft" matzoh balls that sit in our bellies for days, brisket, and fattening desserts?

Wouldn't trade it for a healthy salad any day…

Blintzes for Break the Fast

Recently, I had minor foot surgery and I was unable to do the food shopping, cooking and other "wifely" duties.

My husband rallied to the call and became "the chief cook and bottle washer."

I asked him to buy a cantaloupe for me when he went to the market one afternoon. When he returned home with a large very nice-looking cantaloupe, I was pleasantly surprised. I cut it in half, scooped out the seeds and tasted a piece. It was delicious.

"J*erry, this is terrific. How did you know to buy one so sweet and ripe?"*

"I remembered what you do. You press on the skin with your thumbs to see if it's ripe, and then you smell it. So I did that."

"Jerry, you can't smell anything. You never can."

"I know I can't smell anything, but I did it anyway. I always watch you do it."

We started to laugh, and he reminded me of the time I mimicked my mother's method of making blintzes.

One day I decided to make blintzes using my mother's recipe. I had the cheese mixture prepared and it was time to fry the *bletlechs* (crepes). I put dishtowels all over the kitchen table in preparation for the *bletlechs* to cool down after frying.

I fried the batter, draining the excess batter from the frying pan and walked over to the kitchen table where I turned over the frying pan and began banging it on the table so that the batter would fall out on the dishtowel as a nicely formed crepe.

My husband started to yell from another room, *"What are you doing...banging the pan like that on the kitchen table? You'll dent the table, for cryin' out loud."*

"I am getting the batter out. My mother always did it this way. She banged the frying pan on the table and the bletlech fell out."

"Your mother never had Teflon. She used a cast-iron skillet. Just turn the pan over."

I never realized that. I turned the pan over on my next "run;" and sure enough, the batter slipped out.

We both started to laugh. I was using my mother's recipe and remembering how she used to make the blintzes. Jerry did the same thing. He bought the cantaloupe and checked it out the way I always do. It was a learning experience for both of us.

Many times I find a recipe card in my recipe box and recognize my mother's handwriting. It brings back so many memories. I can smell the banana bread baking in the oven. I can smell the brisket simmering in her "special" sauce. I can see her standing with her blue apron around her waist.

They are wonderful memories. It's *Yom Kippur* soon. I will remember her "break fast" dishes. One of them was her blintzes.

May you be Inscribed for a Year of Good Health and Happiness...

Let's Discuss the High Holidays...

I love to be in temple for the shofar blasts. Don't you just *kvell* when the individual delegated to blow the shofar stands up and holds the shofar to his lips? The ram's horn is so difficult to blow, and you hold your breath until he's through with the final *tekia*.

There have been years when I was more exhausted than the one blowing the shofar. I was praying and holding my breath through those nine staccato notes of the *terua*, hoping he'd get them out without a problem. Do you know that in some synagogues the total number of shofar blasts is one hundred? That is one exhausted *bluzer* (blower) at the end of the service.

Do you know that wearing leather apparel on Yom Kippur is banned? It is considered a pleasurable activity and not to be enjoyed on the sober day of Yom Kippur. Sorry, ladies, put those leather suits and leather shoes back in the closet. Sneakers should be worn. That's fine with me. I can't walk in high heels anyway. Three other activities are banned as well according to the holy books: bathing, eating and sexual intercourse. Bathing? Sorry, but I intend to bathe before coming to temple for the sake of my fellow congregants. Eating? It's not so terrible if I lose a little weight by abstaining for one day. Sexual intercourse? "I take the fifth," but it doesn't sound too bad to me.

Do you know one of the reasons the Kol Nidre prayer is chanted three times is so that latecomers will have a chance to hear it? I guess if you're late, you listen to it through the audio system in the foyer but at least you hear that magnificent melody.

Herring, *salty* herring is supposed to be served at the conclusion of Yom Kippur's fast to induce thirst. Let's be honest, do we need a reason to want water after fasting twenty-four hours? By the end of the service, I feel like I've traveled through the Sahara desert, parched throat and all, and my head is pounding with a miserable headache.

And, at the end of the *Neila* service (the fifth and final), the shofar blower is called upon again to blow one long, long, long blast to signify the end of fasting and to express the feeling that the congregants are exhausted enough and have looked within themselves to want to reach out and to want to make the coming year a better year. Sounds good to me…Happy New Year…May it be a Healthy, Peaceful, and Prosperous Year for one and all……..

Where's a Good Chinese Restaurant?

December 25th is an important date in the Julian calendar. It is Christmas. All the stores are closed. Gentile families gather around the trees, open presents, sit down to a big family dinner, and the Jews stand around saying, "I wonder if there's any restaurants open."

In the northeast, Chinese restaurants are the place to go. All the other restaurants are closed so that employers and employees can have the day off and be together with their families. Down south, there really isn't a terrific Chinese restaurant. So, where do the Jews go?

December 25th was my parents' anniversary, so we always had a big dinner. We ordered in Chinese food or I cooked a turkey, usually the former. The family was always together. However, as time went by, my sister and her family left during Christmas week to go skiing in New Hampshire, and then it was only my two sons and my parents.

Time stops for no one, and my younger son stopped coming home during that vacation season because he needed the time at graduate school to finish papers and to study for term exams. Now there were my parents, my older son and his family, my husband and myself. We went from sixteen plus or minus a child to six adults.

In 1995 we became five when my father passed away. An anniversary cake was no longer necessary. Following that, my mother ended up in a nursing home and the holiday was never the same.

One constant remained. Jerry and I still had Chinese food on Christmas day.

Now we are living in Florida. My family is scattered throughout the states, and I can't find a good Chinese restaurant. And, talk about Christmas being different...especially this year.

Did you ever see Christmas lights (and they are gorgeous) on Royal Palm trees in a climate of eighty degrees? At night we drive around with the convertible top down looking at beautiful Christmas decorations on homes and on trees. Lights are strung around tree trunks and branches.

And, there are tents on every corner. I thought carnivals were in season. I didn't know which one to go to. I couldn't believe the gentiles down south celebrated Christmas by having carnivals. My husband educated me. Those tents were not for carnivals. They sheltered the Christmas trees from the Florida sun. Go know!! How would a Jewish girl from the northeast know this?

Where's the snow? Does Santa land on people's lawns and ruin the grass? And, Santa Claus must *plotz* in such a warm suit when he delivers his gifts in Florida. I hope he wears light-weight cotton.

What do they leave him for a snack? Iced coffee or iced tea? Lemonade? Surely they don't leave him hot cocoa. How does he get in the house? The fireplace is closed and shuttered. Does he stand on the air conditioning compressor outside the house and climb in through a window? He can't enter that way. The windows are closed because the air conditioning is running.

Boy, I thought the Jews had it rough on Christmas Day with stores and restaurants closed. I mean, we can't even go shopping. Now when I think of Santa having to deal with all these problems, I realize mine are minor. I just want a good Chinese restaurant. Santa needs a landing field and a cooler outfit.

Definitely, Christmas will never be the same. Happy Holidays!!

Chanukah is Around the Corner

Is it time to shop for Chanukah already? For some family members, I will take the traditional way out and give Chanukah gelt. It's easier. Besides, nothing I buy is ever the right size or color or something he or she wanted. My mother-in-law, G-d rest her soul, only gave money for Chanukah. She always said, *"Green goes with everything."*

Holidays can be stressful for some people. To avoid *postal insanity* (waiting in line for hours at the post office), I buy toys ***on-line*** for the grandchildren. First, I go to a toy store and check out the toys from top to bottom. Then I return home, sit down at my computer and order it on the appropriate web site. The gift is shipped and even wrapped if I want to spring for the extra $5.00 for gift wrap.

Buying a present for my husband is impossible at this time in our lives. We've been married 40 plus years. There is nothing he wants that he doesn't have; so what can I buy him? *Gornisht (nothing).* We've decided Chanukah is for the *kinder (children),* and we don't make ourselves crazy shopping for something neither one of us wants or needs.

He has shirts he hasn't even worn; underwear is not considered a gift; it's a necessity. Jewelry? Are you kidding? That's something he could buy for me. I never tire of jewelry. I'm even willing to grow an extra appendage to accommodate any gold or diamond bracelet he'd like to see on my wrist.

Gelt is a good gift for the postman, newspaper delivery person, hairdresser, manicurist, anyone who "services" or does something special for us. I get so many new dollar bills at the bank that it begins to feel like monopoly money when I start giving it out as presents. The bank even knows me on a personal level. *"Here she comes again asking for new tens."* I always have *extra* "new money" around because I always remember someone at the last minute to whom I haven't given a present.

Gift giving was not always an eight-day tradition. In Eastern Europe, it was only celebrated on the fifth night and only Chanukah gelt was given out. However, when Jews and Christians associated more with one another, we adopted the tradition of giving gifts as well as gelt. I'm sure the retailers were delighted we went that route.

Well, have to go on line now to decide which Barbie doll I should send to Abby, my granddaughter.

"Jew Year Resolutions"

The old year, Tishrai, 5762, ended and we are in the year 5763, according to the Jewish calendar. To those of us who attended Hebrew school and paid no attention during classes, it means we are leaving the year, 2002, and entering the year, 2003.

How different we celebrate the Jewish New Year in comparison to the Julian New Year. We contemplate our sins over the Jewish New Year, *Rosh Hashanah;* and, we try to forget our sins over the Julian New Year.

We eat heavy Jewish food and drink sweet wine during *Yontif* but we eat in a Chinese restaurant or in a gourmet establishment and drink martinis, expensive wine and champagne on December 31st.

We celebrate the Jewish holidays with our family but we celebrate New Year's Eve with our friends.

We make all kinds of promises *to G-d* over the Jewish holidays but we make resolutions *to ourselves* over the Julian New Year.

Do you know the most common resolutions a person makes on New Year's Eve? To stop smoking and to lose weight. Well, I already stopped smoking and I've been working on the weight situation for years. I find it rather ludicrous when I make this resolution every New Year's Eve, after eating a three course meal, but I set that goal anyway.

If I look back at the resolutions I set for myself last year, I don't think I did such a good job of keeping them.

Some of my resolutions were:

      I promise to be nice to Sarah…but she's such a *nudnick,* wanting to know everything and telling nothing. Don't you know those same people?

I promise not to eavesdrop in a restaurant. Oh right, then I'll have nothing to write about in the column.

I promise to smile whenever my husband says he wants to go food shopping with me…oy!

I promise to stop forwarding e-mails even if it means I break the "chain of good luck," and the sky will fall on my head.

I promise to go to temple more often to make up a minyan.

I promise not to beep at the car in front of me even though the car doesn't move when the light turns green.

I promise not to use my cell phone as an added appendage.

I promise to be more open-minded and accepting of constructive criticism.

I promise to forgive and to forget…Oh, forget this one altogether !!

I promise to be a supportive and loving wife, a loving mother and a loving grandmother…but these are not promises. These are *givens*. They are an ingrained part of any mother and grandmother.

Now remember when you make your resolutions, make them realistic. You don't want to, *chas v'chalilah*, (make the same mistakes again).

This was written via e-mail to my friends in Marblehead, Massachusetts, my first Passover in Florida....

Hi Gang:

As you all know, I went to a friend's home for Passover. I asked what I could do to help. She told me I could either *do desserts* or prepare the Sedar Plate.

It took me two seconds to say, *"I'll do desserts."* I figured that is the easy way out. Wrong !!

I had no intention of baking so I inquired where to buy "real Passover" pastries. I was told the place to go was to Flakowitz's Bakery in Boca Raton. I went there early on Tuesday morning, the day of the Sedar; and, I mean, I went *early.*

When I arrived, at sunrise, there was a line outside the bakery a mile long. I didn't know where the line began or where the line ended. It looked like the line began in Boca and ended in Tampa. When I finally reached the doorway, after G-d knows how many hours of standing in line outside the bakery, I received a number. Imagine, receiving a number just to *enter* the bakery.

Of course, don't forget there are thousands of Jews in southern Florida...and they were all in line with me.

The owners of the bakery hired a guard to keep everyone in line. *Ech mir* a guard. He was probably 110 years old and could hardly stand. What were they expecting from hundreds of Jews waiting to buy bakery goods? A stampede? And, this guard, believe me, would have been trampled one, two, three.

While waiting in line, I began a conversation with an elderly lady. She told me that she had hired a driver for $15.00 an hour to drive her to the bakery. I told her I'd charge her $10.00 an hour to take her home and even walk her upstairs. She laughed. I was serious.

When I was finally allowed entrance, there were two hundred other *Yentas* in there. I was standing at the back of the store listening to people shouting, *"That looks dry. I hope you have more in the back. I want the middle piece. What kind of fruit is in the middle?"*

I stepped on people to get to the counter to see what was displayed in there. It truly was a plethora of assorted Passover baked goods that I have never before seen. The sight was so breathtaking it belonged on the cover of a gourmet magazine. This was truly New York style baked goods.

They had sponge cake on the counter for customers to taste. Some people were making a meal of it. All they needed was a cup of coffee.

It was an experience not to be forgotten and not to be repeated. I called my friend as soon as I returned home and told her next year I'll prepare the Sedar plate.

Happy, healthy Passover to all...

A postscript to this e-mail: This year, 2003, I am getting together with some neighbors in my community. Guess what course I was assigned? You guessed.

Here we go again...

Whose House this Year?

Thanksgiving is around the corner. Has anyone in your family volunteered to host the dinner? *Someone* in the family has to be the *fall guy*.

In my family, my sister always hosts Thanksgiving; of course, she does Rosh Hashanah and Passover as well.

Thanksgiving is relatively easy compared to Passover. Passover is the tough meal to plan since every dish requires matzoh as an ingredient. It is also the meal that stays with us forever. (*G-d bless matzoh and its effects on our digestive system*)

On Thanksgiving turkey is served. That is a *given,* and cranberry sauce as a side dish. Turkey and cranberry sauce is like brisket and *tsimmis.*

Every year the seating is different at Thanksgiving. Some members of our family pass away, and others are born to take their place at the table. Children grow up, get married, and now holiday dinners must be shared with "the other side," the spouse's side. One year the children must go to the *husband's side*; and another year, the children go to the *wife's side.*

Lately, some parents (Who else would host fourteen or more at dinner? The children?) have decided it is easier to take the group out for Thanksgiving dinner. Every restaurant or country club hosts a special meal at holiday times, and it is so much easier on the hostess. Number one: she does not have to get up at 5:00 a.m. to put the turkey in the oven.

Number two: she doesn't have to have the house look *just so*. Number three: she can enjoy herself as much as the guests.

But does dining outside the home lose some of the intimacy, some of the joviality? How can the *little ones* run around? How can you talk about someone? That person might be at the next table. How can you tell the men to go downstairs and watch the football game while the women remain at the table to *kibbitz?*

My feeling is this: I only wish my family were down here in Florida to sit at my dining room table and share the Thanksgiving meal with my husband and me. It would be my pleasure to *serve* them and share the special time. They wouldn't even have to cook a thing.

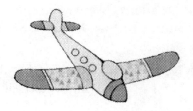

Small Plane Travel is Not for This Jewish Mother

One day in May, 1999, I talked to G-d, Elijah, and any Jewish Prophet whose name came to mind.

I offered the Prophet Elijah my house, my car, and my jewelry to get me through the twin engine airplane ride I had to take to get to my son's graduation. The Prophet Elijah is known to be "always at hand to comfort the sorrowful, cheer the despondent, and help those in distress." I was in distress.

This saga begins when my husband, my older son, Brad, and I arrived at Boston's Logan Airport in torrential rains and catastrophic winds. We were to fly from Boston to Atlanta, Georgia; change planes and fly into Augusta, Georgia, one very small horse and buggy town. We were going to attend my younger son's graduation from the Medical School of Georgia.

I do not love flying but there was no way *this* Jewish Mother was going to miss her son's graduation from medical school.

I began my conversation with Elijah at 11:00 a.m. when we were told that hail was coming down the size of golf balls in Atlanta, and half of Atlanta was without power, a meteorological nightmare.

Our departure time was delayed hour after hour until a *window* in the weather conditions opened. We *cruised* at 33,000 feet above ground. *Why do they even tell us the altitude? Who needs to know?* My husband and son slept the entire trip. I could not close my eyes.

When we arrived in Atlanta, we had 25 minutes to make our connection. If we missed it, we would miss the last flight of the day to Augusta.

Running through the terminal, we arrived at the gate and had to walk *down* a flight of stairs onto the field in the pouring rain.

I see, in front of me, a plane, the size of a model aircraft, with two propellers, and I am supposed to squeeze into this mechanical toy and fly to Augusta. **Oy Gevalt**!!

There are sixteen rows. We are in the last two.

The *piece de re'sistance* was the pilot shouting (no loudspeaker system) that two people are needed to sit up front to balance the airplane since the luggage was in the back. I turned around in my seat, and there, sure enough, was the luggage, slightly hidden by a hanging cloth.

My elder son was watching me since he knew I was walking a fine line between sanity and insanity at this point.

We took off, and I began my earnest conversation with G-d. Never have I talked to G-d so much in my life. I promised him title to our home, our cars, our savings, whatever he wanted.

We hit turbulence and the pilot yelled out, "*Spill the coffee on the floor so you don't burn yourself...and strap yourself in.*" It wasn't coffee I was worried about spilling. We actually landed safe and sound thirty of the longest minutes later. The departing passengers looked like characters from an episode of *Casper the Ghost*.

Would you believe our luggage was not on the plane? It arrived the next morning at our hotel *one hour before* graduation.

I can no longer continue this article since I have to send my computer to The Prophets c/o Elijah. Yes, I promised them the computer as well.

You Call This a Vacation?

Years ago the place to go was *the Catskills*.

Everyone ran to hotels such as the Nevele, the Concord, Kutcher's, Grossinger's, and Brown's. You vacationed there because the hotel was beautiful and clean, the activities were non-stop, the entertainment was wonderful, and the food was plentiful. The waiters *threw* plates of herring, gefilte fish, and platters of lox at you as if lox were fifty cents a pound; and, even then, nova lox cost a lot of money. The rooms were clean and spacious and overlooked the mountains or the pool.

One summer I decided I wanted to go somewhere different. I wanted to go to a quaint inn on an island. Jews did not frequent inns in those days. I knew I would never bump into another Jew in an inn and play Jewish geography. We decided to take a long weekend, travel by ferry to visit Martha's Vineyard.

Martha's Vineyard is a "charming" island that houses many "quaint" inns. But, do you know what "quaint" really means?

In my experience, Quaint means:

The room is tiny. You cannot maneuver a 360 degree turn without tripping over or bumping into the corner of the bed.

The dresser is the size of a dime so there is no room on the top to place a bottle of perfume, a man's wallet or your jewelry.

The bureau is two feet long with three old wooden decrepit drawers that fall on the floor when you pull them open; and there is no runner on the side or bottom of the dresser to put them back correctly. No way would you want to place and ruin your clothes in that decrepit bureau drawer with splinters of wood sticking out from the bottom and sides.

There is no shelf in the bathroom to place your hair dryer; and, when you use the hair dryer, it keeps shutting off because there is not sufficient power in the outlet.

Your cosmetics must *live* on the window shelf in the bathroom or sit on the floor.

There is no telephone but you have your cell phone; however, there is no outlet or stand for the charger.

There is no television. The radio-alarm clock rarely works…even as an alarm.

There may or may not even be air conditioning in the inn, although you have central air conditioning in your own home.

You hear people in the next room talking…at *all* hours. The bed is a double. You have a king-size bed at home. You have never slept so close to your spouse in years. His snoring, his morning breath, he's all over the bed.

Your room has a breath-taking view overlooking the gravel parking lot.

How *charming and quaint*.

The floorboards squeak. The mirror is warped and minuscule. It is positioned awkwardly on the wall so that you can only see your chest. If you kneel, you can see your face. You cannot see what you are wearing. The clothes you donned could be inside out or hanging to the floor.

The breakfast is cold cereal, blueberry muffins, some fruit and coffee.

This is quaint? Quaint, *shmaint!* Give me the Catskills. I'm ready to have food thrown at me. Give me a good corned beef sandwich or a piece of brisket. Cucumber sandwiches and scones don't do it for me.

Better yet, give me a cruise......!

"I Need a Vacation after a Vacation"

Packing is mind boggling, and traveling is exhausting. I know since we drove to Massachusetts from Florida a few weeks ago. Imagine a week of touring and traveling in the car with your spouse for six days straight. It's amazing we're still talking to one another.

"Be careful...not so fast...go slower," and that's Jerry talking to *me*.

Do you know there is a Hebrew prayer for travelers?

An acquaintance of mine told me she would recite the prayer at minyan when she knew we were flying overseas. I asked her to recite that passage for me *whenever* I take a vacation or travel by airplane. I talk to G-d on the airplane anyway. I talk to him before take-off, during the flight, and I kiss the ground and thank him again upon arrival at my destination. Some passengers walk around me; some kiss the ground beside me.

Packing for a trip begins weeks ahead of the actual date. Weeks before our trip I write down everything I want to take, and two days before departure I go through my closet *like Sherman went through Atlanta*. I am the "Queen" of organization.

I pack a large amount of vitamins and medicines, and I always worry that I will be stopped at a security checkpoint and be accused of smuggling drugs. The pills and vitamins are so colorful: red ones, white ones, blue ones. I even sound like a dealer. I pack *Advil, Zantac, Immodium, Tylenol, Sudafed, and Cold-eeze*, to name just a few.

Choosing outfits makes me *meshugah*. Should I take a jacket if it's cool and/or should I take a sweater if there is air conditioning in the restaurants? Sneakers, if my feet hurt from walking? Sandals, if it warms up? A hat, if I go to the beach? I must take an umbrella. Should I take sunscreen lotion as well? There are so many *ifs*.

Have you ever taken a cruise? You can take a cruise to almost anywhere; maybe not to Nebraska or Idaho but you can take a cruise to almost any European country. And, do you know you can travel on a ship with Kosher or even *Glatt* Kosher foods? You can have Kiddush services and daily minyans. There is a Passover trip to Walt Disney World, and a kosher vacation at Club Med in Ixtapa, Mexico for Jewish singles.

I decided the best vacation is to remain at home and to *tell* everyone you will be traveling. Put on the telephone answering machine and *veg out*. Watch TV, read a good book, eat bon-bons…a week later, put on the computer, go to www.Jewishtours.com and take a "Virtual Tour of Israel."

You can tell everyone you went to Israel!! Isn't that easier than coming home with three loads of laundry and with a head cold caught from the passenger sitting beside you on the airplane? Not a bad idea, is it?

I Travel with Two Dresses

Did I ever tell you about the time I went to a wedding in New York? Well, since that momentous event I now travel with *two* dresses.

Let me explain.

I went to the wedding of the son of a dear friend. Four couples traveled from Boston to New York. When we arrived early in the day we sat at the pool, *yented* with everyone and lounged around the pool. Later in the afternoon we went to our respective rooms to dress for the wedding.

I took my new dress from the closet, and I looked it over carefully. There were no wrinkles. This was one new classy dress. I wanted to look *smashing*.

I showered, blow-dried my hair, and put on my underpants. No bra was needed for this dress. The dress was strapless, and the bra was "built in."

I spent an hour in front of the mirror applying my make-up with care.

I stepped into my strapless dress *very* carefully, and it felt *a little* snug. I asked Jerry, my husband, to zip me in the back. He began to pull up the zipper…and it wouldn't budge.

"Jerry, come on. What's the matter?"

"Phyllis, did you try this on in the store after alterations?"

"No, I was in a hurry."

"It won't zip."

"What are you talking about? Pull it up!"

"I'm pulling, Phyllis. It's not moving."

I began to *lose my cool*. What do I do? I can't get into the dress. I can't go in shorts or in a bathing suit to a wedding. I'll stay in the room.

Jerry gathers my friends from their rooms to our room to convince me to go to the wedding. They are going to figure something out.

I have seven people, seven *mayven* watching me have an anxiety attack because I can't get into the *far-shtunk-in-eh* dress. My friend's husband, Arthur, says not to worry. He will gently try to pull up the zipper. He pulls and pulls and *zziiippp*...the zipper breaks.

The dress falls to the floor. I am not wearing a bra, and my friends are as aghast as I am. I quickly pull up the dress and am standing there ready to faint. I start to *shvitz* from aggravation, my make-up starts to run, and I need to shower all over again. My perfectly blown-dried hair starts to look not-so perfect.

"I'm not going. I'll stay in the hotel room."

"You can't stay in the hotel room. We'll sew you up in the dress."

"What? I won't even be able to get out of it to go to the bathroom."

"So, go to the bathroom now, 'cause we're going to sew you in it."

I won't talk money but this dress cost a small fortune, and I am being sewn into it. Now, you can imagine what the back of the dress looked like with Donna, my friend, basting me in the dress. She's a real estate broker, not a seamstress. She is lucky she can sew a button, and she is sewing me into a designer gown.

The back of the dress looked like hell. The stitching was stretched across my bare skin in an attempt to hold the dress closed, in lieu of the zipper. Another friend, watching this fiasco, had a beautiful matching shawl with her dress. I offered her my house and children if I could wear her shawl over my dress. She agreed with tears in her eyes although she refused the gift of my children.

Meanwhile, the hostess, our friend, is at the wedding wondering *where is everyone*? The bus is waiting downstairs at the hotel to take us to the reception, and it is the last hired bus for the evening.

We go on the bus. I'm afraid to move, laugh, cry, do anything, or the basting will rip…and I'll be standing in a dress around my ankles with underpants and no bra.

It is probably the hottest day of the summer, no air conditioning in the hall, and I am wearing a shawl over a dress. I don't think I danced all night. I know my friends were snickering every time they looked at me since I was *shvitzing* in the dress with the basting and the shawl.

That was an evening To Forget. Now you know why I travel with two dresses to any out-of-town affair. Oy, the BocaYente will never forget that night.

"A Walk and a Half"

According to the *Sun Sentinel*, a Miami based newspaper, a Buddhist monk completed a seven-year walking journey. The Buddhist priest, dubbed the *Marathon Monk,* finished a ritual that took seven years and covered a distance that equaled a trip around the world. He wore only a flowing robe and flimsy straw sandals.

He did not take any form of transportation. He walked the entire journey. *Ken-a hora* !!

I can not imagine taking a trip wearing only a robe and sandals. First of all, I only wear my robe when I'm sick and I'm walking around the house. I would never let people see what I look like in my robe. And, I don't even own straw sandals. They must irritate the feet terribly.

This monk carried only candles, a prayer book and a sack of vegetarian food. I would carry a cell phone, money, and my pills and vitamins. Oh, I'd carry water too. His regimen was exhausting. He ran, he prayed 250 times a day (we are lucky when we get a minyan twice a day); and he had to chant mantras for nine days without food, water, or sleep. Give me a break! How did he do it? What sheer will and determination. But *why* did he do it? The article never gave any specific reason other than it is a ritual.

Now Jewish people go on journeys and we have more than enough rituals. We certainly have one of the most popular religious journeys. It's called *Let's Go Israel,* and it is one of the first things our children hear when they start to walk and talk.

How many of our children visited Israel at sixteen years of age, when it was considered safe to visit Israel? I know mine did and they still talk about the trip to this day. Of all the trips my husband and I have taken, our visit to Israel remains the most vivid…and beloved.

The monk took quite a journey. AARP would never advertise in the Elderhostel pamphlet for this trip, and not many individuals would have the fortitude to even contemplate it. I couldn't even consider it. *Seven years* shlepping around with only the clothes on my back. It's exhausting enough to go away for a week. I commend this Buddhist Monk.

THE CHILDREN

HERE COME THE CHILDREN!!!!!!!

Vacation week in Florida begins by picking up the children at the airport.

They have their luggage, car seats, carriages, diapers, and toys…and we, the grandparents, have extra car seats, carriages, diapers, and toys.

Here they come…

"*Papa, Grandma,*" and into our arms they fly. Welcome to south Florida, the winter home of Jewish snowbirds. The west coast of Florida has Jewish snowbirds as well, but that's supposed to be a classified secret.

Oy, we're so excited (let us remember this sacred moment throughout the week when we can hardly stand or function).

The children are here…

Gallons of *Tide* detergent are brought into the laundry room, extra shampoo and soap is ready, and towels are standing by for use over and over and over.

Use it once, put it in the laundry room is the credo our children live by; it is not necessarily the credo they live by in **their** own home.

The refrigerator is bursting with fresh fruit, orange juice, *Coca-Cola*, you name it. The refrigerator is actually *sweating* from overuse. The door is like a revolving door. The *little ones* stand there and decide what they want to eat while the food is *sweating*. The older children eat anything that isn't moving.

You have vowed to close your eyes when your grandchildren sit on the white furniture eating snacks, and you turn a deaf ear when your children have a tiff.

The sun is an important factor at vacation time. They all love to go to the pool; yet, the ever familiar line, *"Let's go to the Flea Market"* will be spoken at some time during the week; usually, on the first rainy day.

The roads in Florida during vacation week are like the Daytona Speed Track *without* the speed. There are three times as many cars, all driving in the left lane and not knowing when and where they should turn left or right.

Where are these cars going? To Friday night services at Temple? They are going to a *restaurant,* of course!! Hundreds of families are going to hundreds of restaurants, all at the same time; and every restaurant is mobbed.

"How long do we have to wait?" you ask the hostess.

"Not long, maybe 45 minutes."

The 45 minutes usually turns into an hour-and-a-half but it's better than cooking. You are exhausted, and you have laundry waiting for you.

Was it really last week you were counting the days till the children arrived?

The week is over. The children had a wonderful time. You are totally wiped out and need a week to recuperate. Now you are driving the *kinder* to the airport.

They loved it. They had a ball.

"Grandma, Papa, we can't wait for next year."

"*Ma, Dad, thanks for everything. The kids loved it and so did we. We're going to make reservations for next year as soon as we get home.*" (*Oy gevalt !!* I'm thinking maybe I should leave the key under the mat and go for a cruise with my husband.)

"*Children, have a safe and comfortable flight.*"

Their plane takes off. They promise to call when they arrive home. You know what? You'll be just as excited next year waiting for their plane to arrive as you were this year.

You'll be waiting for the "*Papa, Grandma, we're here!*" resounding in the airport. They're your children, and you love them unconditionally…as long as you don't have to *live* with them for more than one vacation week at a time. It's nice when they come, and it's nice when …

Have to take a nap now; they just left.

My Children Trust Me with their House Keys

My children trust me with their house key. I have their alarm code as well. I would never betray their trust and enter their home without their knowing. I would never *nose around* their home as well.

You know something? I don't want to know what's behind their closed doors. I have enough *tzorus* and hidden secrets behind my own doors.

I have clothes in my closet that could hang a little straighter. I have shoes that are not all in a row. I have personal papers they need not know about. So, why would I want anyone to look in *my* closet?

Yet, I remember my mother and my mother-in-law, when they babysat for my children at my house, maybe 35 years ago, didn't leave a door unopened, a drawer closed or a stone unturned.

They went through my house faster than *Sherman marched through Atlanta*. They were more thorough than any cleaning woman I ever had in my home. And, they weren't cleaning…they were peeking. They were looking.

Was I a good housekeeper? Were my clothes folded?

And, they weren't shy about their *trespassing.* My mother certainly wasn't. She left notes !!!

Can you imagine if we did that to our children? It's enough we have to tiptoe around them when we want to *tell* them something.

Yes, my mother left me notes!

"Phyllis, you could fold your clothes neater."

"Don't put the bananas in the refrigerator. They'll turn brown."

"You could vacuum a little better in your son's room."

And, so on and so on…

It never failed. I would return from a mini-vacation after my parents baby-sat for my kids, and I knew the notes would be waiting for me.

It was a trade-off: the notes for their babysitting. I took the notes. They got their time with the grandchildren. I got some quiet time with my husband, and as an added bonus, I also got the *notes*!!

My children are grown, and now I am the grandmother. Can you imagine if I did that today?

That's suicide. (By the way, my daughter-in-law is an excellent housekeeper and wife and mother.)

'Hak mir nit kain tcheinik'

(How do you explain this to a gentile?)

Literally, it means "Don't chop me a teapot.

Figuratively, it means, "Don't bother me."

When we left Florida at the end of May, I asked my son, Michael, who lives in Atlanta, if he was planning to visit us in Marblehead this summer.

Evidently, it was not the first time I asked him this question; and, I did not know he had already purchased tickets to surprise us with a visit this summer.

Michael is not exactly steeped in the Yiddish language but he does know some Yiddish expressions, and his answer to me was, "*Hak mir nit kain tcheinik.*" The literal translation is *Don't bang on the tea kettle*. What he really wanted to say was "*Enough already. Stop bothering me.*"

In other words, I said it *once* and he heard me. I said it *twice*, he heard me and ignored me; but by the *third* time, he heard me, ignored me, and didn't want to hear me again. The expression refers to a tea kettle whistling and perking before the tea (hot water) is out of the tea pot. If it *klops* so much it becomes a banging headache.

As an example, I remember asking my husband in our earlier years, "*Did you call your mother?*"

His answer: *"Not yet. I will."*

Ten minutes later: *"So, did you call your mother yet?"*

His reply: *"I told you I will."*

"Today, tomorrow, next week!?"

"I will call my mother when I am through reading this page."

"So how long is the page? You can't stop there and go back to what you were reading? The book is so important?"

"I am in the middle of a good part."

"The book is more important than your mother?"

Phyllis, "Don't hak mir a tcheinik." He called his mother.

He couldn't take the "nagging" anymore. He knew I could continue for days on end.

"So, Jerry, was it so terrible to call your mother and just say hello? Some day you'll hope your kids will call you."

(It's scary but the day is actually here)

"Jerry, did the kids call?"

Children, if you are reading this, I hope you don't feel any guilt; although, I did raise you so that you would feel *some* pangs of remorse.

Returning to the interrogation of my son, about his visiting us in the summer, I didn't get angry at Michael when he told me to stop *haking him a tcheinik*. It didn't sound so terrible in Yiddish, and I was glad to know he still remembered one or two expressions.

Anyway, *A vue shtet geschreiber* (where is it written) that I can't *hak him a tcheinik*? Guilt and *hakking* are in my Jewish genes. It's my heritage. My mother taught me well.

"Kislev was Good to Me"

This is the month of Kislev, the ninth of the twelve months of the Jewish calendar. It is the month of Chanukah and derives from the Hebrew word for "security" and "trust." Kislev is the month in which the inner portion of the Torah was given on Mount Sinai.

In the Gregorian calendar it is the month of November; and, in that month are two very important birthday dates. Both my sons were born in November.

Today, publication date, November 8, is my younger son's birthday.

I can remember his earlier birthday parties better than I can remember what I did yesterday. Can't you remember events that happened years ago far better than you can remember what you did last week?

There are days when I can't remember what I had for dinner the previous evening. I've walked into a room and forgotten why I walked into that room. I have lists everywhere. I have them on my refrigerator, on my desk, near my computer, every possible place. I have three calendars; yes, three. One small pocket calendar for my car so that I can carry it into the hairdresser or into the doctor's office; another calendar hangs on my refrigerator, and one sits on my desk saying, *"Phyllis' Busy Week."*

If I couldn't find one of those calendars I wouldn't know where to go and when.

Yet, I remember my son's Little League games 30 years ago. He was always the one up at bat when his team was one run behind the other team. It was the last inning, there were two outs, and the whole team was counting on him.

He was *plotzing* and so was I. My heart was in my mouth; and I knew, and he knew, he was going to strike out. He just hadn't notified his teammates that, unless a miracle occurred, his bat would never make contact with that ball. It never did. Sports were not his thing.

The closest thing to sports that he enjoyed was shooting "hoops" in our driveway and bike riding. He rode his bicycle to school almost every day. In the winter he wore a plaid hat with ear flaps, and I would say to him, *"Do you know what you look like in that hat?"*

He didn't care. He was warm. And, to this day, I don't know where he found that hat. I swear I didn't buy it for him.

One *spring* day he came in the house after school *wearing mittens.* I asked if there were a snowstorm somewhere in Marblehead and I hadn't been aware of this weather disturbance. He said the mittens were in the pocket of his jacket so he thought he should wear them.

I remember so many funny stories about this son of mine. He is the "absent-minded professor" in my book. He is also one of the brightest, warmest pediatricians in the state of Georgia, and a humanitarian to the core.

Today, he is one year older. I still have the privilege of worrying about him. In three weeks my other son will be a year older. I have the privilege of worrying about him as well.

I'm a Jewish mother, and it goes with the territory. I have wrinkles and gray hair from these sons of mine, but I also have many laugh lines.

Happy birthday, Michael…and soon, a happy birthday to you, Brad.

So you see, the month of Kislev is very important to me. I received two wonderful blessings that month. (Don't tell them I said that. They'll never let me live it down).

"Call Me When You Get There"

Do you remember when your children were younger and you asked, *"Call me when you get there."* They could be traveling by car, train, airplane or even bicycle, and you would say, *"Call me when you get there."* Their telephoning you meant it was O.K. to stop the *Worry Meter* in your head.

You always worried about their traveling even if they were bicycling to a friend's house...and G-d forbid, they forgot to call; you imagined the worst.

My children, when they traveled by airplane, got wiser in their comments as they got older, *"Well, if I don't get there, you'll know. Just watch the T.V."* I did not, nor do I today, think that is funny.

I used to call their home when I thought they should be home. I tried to calculate the E.T.A.: *"Let's see...their plane got in on time at 8:00 (I called the flight line); they need time to pick up their luggage, drive home, and they should be walking in the door now.* **"Hello?"**

"Hi, Mom. I'm walking in the door. I'm home. You timed it right again."

Wise guy, he saw my name on the caller I.D.

Cell phones and e-mailing have added a new dimension to traveling. People can call directly from the airport to announce they have arrived safely or they can call from the car in which they are traveling, "*Hi, Mom, I'm driving through New York. Do you want me to call you when I enter Connecticut or should I just leave the telephone line open and you can join us in the car ride?*"

When my son, at the age of 24, traveled through Europe for four months *alone*, I made the stipulation that he must call every Sunday to let me know where he was and how he was. I do not know how I survived those four months, and on the Sunday that he forgot to call, I could have been institutionalized. A million things could have happened between Sundays but I had to receive that telephone call; and, there were times that he just could not get near a telephone.

My husband took it in stride, never worried, and humored me until I did hear from our son. Granted, I was overly *meshugie,* but it couldn't be helped. Worrying is in my genes. It's definitely in the female genes; and, if you're Jewish, you don't have a prayer. You are a *Naturally-Born Worrier.*

Today e-mailing has made my life and many other lives easier. When my son travels in a foreign country he is able to keep in touch by just visiting a computer cafe with e-mail internet capabilities, and we don't have to wait for Sundays. Yes, I still insist on hearing from him once a week even though he is in his thirties. I told you, I am a **worrier**.

What is interesting is the fact that life goes around in cycles. Children now tell their parents to call them when they've arrived safely. When does that start? When parents reach the age of 60? 70? I don't know but it's a *touching* phenomena.

My children have not started asking yet. I am hoping that is because they feel we are *too young* to worry about; G-d forbid, they do not care.

And, there is one other common factor involved in traveling, "*Gey gezunterheit un cuma gezunterheit.*" (go in good health and come in good health)

"Tell Me After"

Children…there's nothing like them. There are some days they make you so proud, and some days they make you so *meshugey*. They have the ability to know what *buttons to push, when to push them and for how long.* You want them to confide in you and tell you stories about their life; and, then there are times you wished you stressed the fact that some things should only be on a *need to know* basis.

My boys grew up in a home where everything was discussed at the kitchen table. There were some times when I lost my appetite during a discussion, but I kept a "poker face" during those times because I am a strong believer in frank and open discussion between parents and children.

At *this* stage in our lives, our children are grown. One son has a wife and two children. He confides in his wife, not us, as is often the case. On the other hand, our other son is a single parent, and we still have open lines of communication.

As a pediatrician associated with Emory University, he travels to foreign countries to help poor, sick children. Last year he visited Haiti and told me stories via e-mail while he was there that I really didn't want to know.

I wanted to know "*after.*" I didn't want to know that he needed an armed guard to accompany him in the jungle (why was he in a jungle?). I didn't want to know that dysentery was *going around* in his camp; and, I certainly didn't want to know that he fell 25 feet down the face of an active volcano on Lake Atitlan.

"*Tell me after…*" I can't worry thousands of miles away. Today with e-mail, I have the ability to worry immediately. I don't have to wait for his return to the states.

I have a friend whose son was traveling on the expressway in a snowstorm. He called his mother on the cell phone to tell her the roads were horrible. Why did he have to tell her? Did her worrying about him *help* him? What is even more unbelievable? He got hit by the car behind him while talking on the phone with her. She heard the whole thing. She was *certifiable* following that cell phone conversation. She heard the crash and the horns blowing. He finally told her he had to hang up because the ambulance was on the way.

How about another friend's son calling his parents from a phone booth in Jerusalem to tell them he couldn't find his group of friends? It was 3:00 a.m. in Marblehead. What did he want his parents to do? Whom could they call at that time? They were frantic. What they didn't know was their son, after hanging up the phone, turned around and there was his group waiting for him. However, he forgot to call his parents back to tell them. That was one long night for two distraught people.

Children, *sometimes*, it's not so terrible: *"Tell us **After**..."*

Matchmaker, Matchmaker, Make <u>Him</u> a Match…

These are the famous or infamous words of Tevya's daughter in *Fiddler On the Roof*. Most everyone is familiar with the words and the melody.

A matchmaker, *shadchan,* was a very important person in earlier times. S*hadchans*, marriage brokers, were given free reign to roam the country while Jews were not allowed to move around the country as freely as gentiles. The *shadchans* were a necessity in the world of wedded bliss.

I played the role of matchmaker twenty-one years ago, and I am happy to say the couple is still together and the grandparents of nine, *ken-a-hora*. But G-d forbid, I should act as matchmaker and suggest a girl's name to my unmarried son. His response is, *"Mom, please…"* He leaves the rest unsaid, but he means *"Leave me alone. I'll find my own dates."*

What, however, is the difference between a matchmaker and www.jdate.com or www.yid.com? These are websites with a computerized *shadchan*. The questionnaire on these sites ask questions that will allow the computer to match likes and dislikes, degrees of education, incomes, etc., with another of the opposite gender. It even offers the prospect, the opportunity to meet someone of the same gender, if he/she wishes. So what's the difference between a *shadchan* and a Jewish website?

Whom do you think suggested all those categories to the administrators of the websites? A Jewish mother, of course, the best stand-in for a real *shadchan*. A mother knows whom she wants her son or daughter to date.

Evidently, one mother was found who sat down with the administrator of *jdate* or some other Jewish dating website and listed the questions that should be asked of those attempting to find a match.

She did not *recommend* attaching a photo but the administrator insisted that some people prefer to see whom they are e-mailing. Let me ask you this: Do you think everyone is honest and sends in his or her real photo? I don't know if I would have years ago. I was the kind of girl who was described as, *She has a nice personality*. Wasn't that nice? G-d only knows what they thought I looked like. I did manage to get married at the ripe old age of twenty-one. My husband is a *keeper* too; and, evidently I am. We've been married for 41years.

What is amazing is the fact that jdate.com is all over the world. They sponsor parties, chat rooms, e-mailing. They make available many avenues of meeting via the internet. Just like a marriage broker, they charge a person to have their profile posted on the membership list.

Don't you wonder if everyone posts a truthful profile? Am I too skeptical of an innocuous computer fixing up my son when I have a list of more than twenty nice Jewish girls from good homes?

Oh well, I guess this is the age of *progress*, and I'm still stuck in the Old World.

But, truthfully, isn't a Jewish website the same as a real live *shadchan?*

And a *shadchan* doesn't **crash** like a computer.

Grandmas No Longer Have Blue Hair

"Hey, Dad! Grandma sent me ten bucks for my birthday!"

"Isn't that sweet?" The world would be a nicer place if it was full of people like your grandma."

"True...but then again, nobody would be able to reach anything on a top shelf."

I read those words in the comic strip *"Zits"* by J. Scott and J. Borgman, and it brought a smile to my lips. Remember when all *bobies* (grandmas) were shorter than you? You could be three feet tall, and they were still shorter.

They all had gray and blue hair; some spoke broken Yiddish (mine did). They always babysat for us, and for some reason they taught us card games. They taught us *"War, Casino, or Fish."* I remember it like yesterday. In fact, I remember it better than I remember what I did yesterday.

I adored my little old grandmother. She always seemed old. We called her *Baba*. Half the time I couldn't understand what she was saying in her broken English and she may not have understood me many times as well. But there was an unspoken love between her and her grandchildren, and we all knew she loved us unconditionally.

She would *shtup* me a few dollars when my mother wasn't looking. Don't think my mother didn't know either. She turned a blind eye. My grandmother left *bupkees* when she passed away, but she left many loving memories with the whole family. No one cared about what she left or how much, if anything.

She didn't drive; in fact no one in the family could drive or even afford a car. *Today's* grandmothers are a different story from the grandmothers of yesterday.

Not only do we drive, but we drive sport cars and convertibles and SUV's.

Blue hair? No way !! We go to the hairdressers religiously. We're blondes and brunettes. We have straightened hair or naturally straight hair. We do not wear pony tails, and we do not drive green Volvos.

We could teach the grandchildren card games but the only ones we play now are canasta and bridge. Some of us play poker with the best of them. I don't think the children would enjoy those card games or mah jongg.

We can golf with the grandchildren and some of us can play tennis with the children.

Best of all, we get to see the newest movies with them, and we can go to "chain" restaurants when they are little, and then we can treat them to the finest of dining when they are older…if they have time for us.

Grandmas don't play computer games but we do e-mail the children when we are away. Grandmas are good for buying clothes, games, theatre tickets, etc., and they are good for wiping away tears and problem solving.

Grandmas love unconditionally…and they're always good for a few bucks…and some of us can reach the top shelf.

I can't…

Being a Grandmother Beats Being a Mother

Being a mother is no easy task. Being a grandmother is a piece of cake.

Being a mother requires driving skills to chauffer the urchins to public school, Hebrew school, and after-school activities. Being a grandmother allows you to take the children to the movies, dinner, and/or shopping…and back to their own home at the end of a day.

Being a mother gives you gray hair. Being a grandmother allows you to touch-up the gray hair you earned being a mother.

Being a mother requires you to say no to ice cream and candy. Being a grandmother allows you to take the kids out for ice cream.

Being a mother requires you to drive the children to their first day at camp and smile all the way home. Being a grandmother allows you to send "care packages" to the children and to their friends at camp.

Being a mother requires you to drive the "gifted ones" to art classes and piano lessons. Being a grandmother allows you to hang their masterpieces on your refrigerator and to cheer wildly at their dancing and piano recitals.

Being a mother requires your cooking three meals a day for the children, cleaning their room, and putting away their toys. Being a grandmother allows you to buy the toys for the mothers to put away at the end of a day.

Being a mother requires you to wash four loads of clothes a day and towels by the dozens. Being a grandmother allows you to buy the clothes that the mothers have to wash.

Being a mother requires you to limit their allowance so that they learn the value of a dollar. Being a grandmother allows you to supplement their allowance with as much *gelt* as you want to give them.

Being a mother enables you to kiss the children when no one is looking for fear of embarrassing them. Being a grandmother allows you to hug and kiss them whenever and wherever.

Being a mother forces you to be a disciplinarian and to set the rules and regulations. Being a grandmother allows you to *bend* the rules and regulations.

Being a mother, you worry about the children. Being a grandmother, you worry about the children and the children's children.

Being a mother allows you to comfort and advise but you don't know if the kids are listening. Being a grandmother allows you to comfort and advise, and you hope they're listening to you *and* their parents.

Being a mother means you must make difficult decisions in life that will affect your children. Being a grandmother means you must support your children when they make their decisions concerning your grandchildren.

I am a mother, and I am a grandmother. I am reaping all the benefits that come with being a grandparent. I actually managed to get through motherhood fairly unscarred.

So remember, mothers:

Being a mother is the first step to being a grandmother. And, it's worth all the aggravation getting to this stage. It's a beautiful place to be...

This Is Retirement?

Living in an Active Adult Community

I called my friend the other day around noon. When she answered the telephone, she sounded as if she were sick or as if she were sleeping.

"Barbara, are you all right?"

"I'm fine, Phyllis. I'm resting between activities."

I laughed out loud and said, "We're at camp. I forgot."

It feels like a day at camp when I awake every day with the sun shining through the bedroom window.

I get up early, letting my husband sleep a little longer so that I can have my *private time.* I read the newspaper in the kitchen, boot up the computer, check my e-mails, *futz* around, look out at the lake and think how fortunate I am to be here.

What is my schedule today?

Early in the morning, I begin my day playing tennis with three other ladies, or take a walk or go down to the clubhouse to lift weights…depends on the day.

In the afternoon, I may have a women's club, mystery club or writing club to attend, or canasta or mah jong…depends on the day.

In the evening, I may have chorus rehearsal or another canasta game with friends. We may be going out to dinner with another couple…depends on the day.

I try to find time to read which I adore, food shop which I deplore, have my hair cut and my nails done, catch up with my e-mail, and lunch with friends who do not live within this *shtetl* (village).

By evening, I usually fall asleep on the couch or in bed with the book open and my glasses falling off my nose. The eleven o'clock news is usually over without my seeing one segment.

This really is camp. Did I forget to say the sunset is magnificent in Florida, and snow does not reflect from the waters of the lake?

My northern friends and family do not understand this lifestyle. They call it *la-la land*. So be it…if it's *la-la land*. It's well deserved after years of hard work. It's the brass ring we caught on the merry-go-round ride. It is sunshine and paradise.

I play tennis with a lovely lady who never wears a watch. She said after she retired, her time was her own. I couldn't live without a watch or I'd be late for my next activity. I love my new camp friends, people I would never know if we hadn't moved down to Florida; and, I, especially love returning to my bunkmate in my beautiful cabin to share all this bliss we worked so hard to have.

Isn't camp wonderful?

"Fill 'er Up?"

Do you remember when you would drive into a gas station and the attendant, neatly groomed and attired, would come up to your car window? You would roll down the window, and he would say to you, *"Fill 'er up?"*

You would answer, *"Yes, please,"* and he would do just that. And while he was filling the car with the hose with the automatic shut-off valve, he returned to your car window and asked, *"Check under the hood?"*

After checking under the hood, as a bonus, he would wash your front and back car windows. And, if you came to the station on the right day in the week, the attendant would give you another drinking glass to add to the others he gave you in the previous weeks. I had to choose between gas station glasses and *Yahrzeit* glasses when I was thirsty.

Not any more…Now you drive up to the gas pump, get out of the car, and *you* become the *Gas Jockey*. I usually don't mind doing filling the gas tank of my car, but today was a "bummer."

Number one: I couldn't figure out which way the card went into the slot.

Number two: The sun was reflecting on the instruction window of the pump, and I couldn't read the instructions.

Number three: the automatic stop was removed so I had to stand and hold the hose handle, and it was hot and humid outside today.

Why do they remove the automatic stop anyway? Who would want to steal it? *"Oh, look, I stole an automatic shut-off valve and they didn't even know at the gas station. Maybe I'll gift wrap it and give it to Jerry for his birthday."* Give me a break!!

After I filled the car, I started to drive away and then I remembered I didn't take the receipt that had my credit card number written on it. I backed up, wished I had seen the dog before I backed up, and went to retrieve the slip. It was in the machine with only the last four numbers written on it, but I had to have it in my possession. I would have worried that my credit card number was out there somewhere...like it isn't already.

I would have washed the car windows but the window washer sponge was missing. Someone must have really stolen that. You know something...I miss that nice man who used to say to me, *"Fill 'er up?"*

The BocaYente Attended an Eastern Star Installation

The installation ceremony reminded me of Olde English theatre productions. The players were instructed to move around the room via *compass directions.*

"You, go to the North. You, go Southwest. You, Rose, go to the East."

I felt like I was in Florida again. They did not say, *"Take a left or a right."* They said, *"Go to the East."*

No individual was referred to by name. They were incognito. They were called Rose, Aster, Lily, names of flowers. I felt as if I were at a horticultural show.

One individual had the name of Esther, a nice Jewish name, for a nice gentile lady.

And, these people paraded around, like you couldn't believe. They marched to the east. They marched to the west. They marched in circles. They marched and they marched…to music, and, at times, to no music. Maybe it was music *they* could only hear. The organist played a march, the choir lady screeched, and again they marched and they marched.

Then they bowed. They bowed and they bowed. They bowed when they met someone. They bowed when they left someone…just a *little* nod of the *kepala* (little head).

They have secrets too. They have a secret clasp of their hands…one fist clenched over the other hand as if in prayer. They didn't give the "bird" though. I watched.

They wore gimp lanyards around their necks. That was the symbol of their position. One had a whistle. She was the gym instructor. Another had a whip. She was the sex instructor, and one had a donut. She was in charge of refreshments.

They were dressed to the *nines*. The men wore tuxedos, and the women wore long swishy dresses that reminded me of costumes from *Amadeus*.

These women sat down, stood up, marched, recited memorized formal verses, and then sat down, stood up, and marched again. I was exhausted watching them parade around. I was also exhausted because it took them two hours to do their sitting and standing and parading around the room.

It's always refreshing to learn about different cultures, different religions, and different ways of life. Now I have witnessed a most different and interesting Masonic installation. I have seen and learned about Eastern Star, and if I'm invited again next year, I'm busy.

I Don't Recognize these People

I am sitting at the computer looking not only at the screen but at photos of children that do not belong to me.

These pictures are situated on the wall directly behind my laptop screen. They are also on the wall behind me as well. They are on the wall of the staircase. They are in my bedroom. *They are everywhere !!*

You see, I am renting a condo that belongs to another couple who travel through the summer…on their houseboat in France, mind you.

It seems as it they have 30 children between them (second marriage); and, combined they must have 60 grandchildren. They must love to look at their families constantly because you can't move one step in this condo without seeing a framed photograph of one of their relatives on any and every wall. They not only have 90 heirs, but sisters and brothers and dead relatives are hanging on many walls. They have photos of their boat as well, and those photos are interesting and unusual.

I placed some framed pictures of *our* family on a table in the living room because I was losing my identity. I was beginning to think of their family as my family, and I was inventing stories about their life. It's strange to live with photos of other children and adults who don't belong to your family. I must admit I removed the photos on the coffee tables and dressers, but I was not about to strip the walls bare of the entire *mishpucha* (family).

I put drawings from my granddaughter on the refrigerator door and moved *their children's Picassos* to the *side* of the refrigerator. I found photos of our family and placed them over the photos of their grandchildren. Yet, I feel like I've gained another family with all the *other* pictures around me.

There have been times when I wasn't so thrilled with my own family, and we all have those days; but now I've gained another family about whom to worry.

I'm looking at a bridal photo now and wondering why I wasn't invited to the wedding. I don't know them, but I feel like I do.

When I leave here in September, I'll miss them, my *new* family, the young ones, the old ones, the pretty ones, the ugly ones, the dead ones. I just hope I remember to return the photos to their rightful place in this unit.

Maybe I'll even leave a photo of my family to show them, *"I have family too, you know. You live with them this winter. I lived with yours this summer."*

This is Dinner Conversation?

My husband and I were having dinner in a lovely Italian restaurant in Boca Raton, and I inadvertently overheard an interesting conversation between two couples at the next table.

The men, at this table, were wearing flowered shirts from the seventies, and the women had enough make-up on to sink a ship.

Their voices were a tad loud, and the four of them were wearing more jewelry than *Tiffany* has in their showcases. The women were hunched over the table as if they had osteoporosis, and their heads were parallel with the table top due to the weight of their necklaces. Their chains must have weighed a ton.

Their arms were hanging immobile at their sides due to the amount of bracelets and rings they were wearing. I was curious to see if they were going to be able to lift their silverware.

I knew they were married to one another. I just knew that. That was a *given*. I was curious, however, whether they were MOT (members of the Tribe).

It took me ten seconds overhearing their conversation to know the answer to that question.

I heard one husband ask the other husband, *"So, what cemetery are you going to be buried in? Where'd you buy plots?"*

Have you ever heard a gentile ask another gentile, *"In what cemetery are you going to be buried?"*

Gentiles don't discuss that subject at dinner. Jews make it the topic of conversation.

Jews have to be buried with the family. We must be together. Why?

When we're alive there are times we don't want to even sit together at the same table.

Have you ever made a Bar Mitzvah or a wedding? Haven't you heard?

"Don't sit me with Estelle. I'm not talking to her...this week."

Estelle could be her sister, cousin, or even her mother. Yet, they want to be buried next to one another when *the time comes*.

Why do Jews want to be buried near each other?

We want to make it convenient for the children to visit our graves. They don't visit us enough when we're alive, but we expect them to visit us when we're dead. So we make it convenient for them. They can visit the whole family at the same time.

Nu, does this make sense? Why do Jewish people discuss their plots...at dinner, no less?

Maybe it's a Jewish idiosyncrasy. So where are yours?

Mine are in Temple Beth El Cemetery on Lowell Street in Peabody, Massachusetts...but I'm in no hurry.

We Did a Mitzvah for the Children

We are back on the North Shore of Boston for the summer.

This past summer Jerry and I made life a little bit easier for our children. We went to the local funeral chapel in our hometown in Massachusetts and planned our funerals. We bought our plots years ago from our temple, Temple Beth El, and we made all the necessary arrangements, even picking out the caskets. Needless to say, I picked out the more expensive one. If this was going to be my final resting place, I was going to be comfortable. I even changed our cemetery plots to the newer section.

Thank G-d, we are both healthy and in a healthy frame of mind, so we decided this is when we should both make the necessary arrangements for our "send-off." When my parents passed away, it was such an emotional undertaking for me that I didn't want my "kids" to be in the same situation. Besides, who knows what I want more than I do?

I knew the newspapers in which I wanted the obituary to appear; I knew whether I wanted certain ritual procedures performed; it turns out my husband was more reformed in his thinking than I was. My children do not know our feelings on this subject. Who sits down to discuss it? We even had to prepare for the eventuality that we may need to be *shipped* up north from Florida. It wouldn't be first class, that's for sure; but there's a service called "minimum shipment." I kept getting confused and calling it "speedy delivery."

We picked "The Religious Merchandise Package." It included acknowledgement cards, candles, grave markers, the whole *shmear*. When it was time to pick out the caskets, I was not exactly thrilled with entering that *particular* room but it was so much easier for me to do than have a loved one perform this uncomfortable task during a traumatic time.

Besides, they probably wouldn't want to spend too much money.

I honestly think we did a *mitzvah* for our children. Not only did they not have to pay for it, but they did not have to deal with making weighty decisions at an emotional time. I honestly recommend this gift, and I suggest doing it when you are healthy and in a healthy frame of mind.

Someday, ***I hope not soon***, my children will appreciate this "gift."

Welcome to the Neighborhood

Our doorbell rang one day last week and I went to answer the door. The peephole is too high in the door, by the way, and I can't even see who is outside, so I have to shout, *"Who is it?"*

"It's Judy, your new neighbor from across the street."

Great, I am finally going to meet my neighbors. I open the door, and there is Judy.

She is standing in the entrance, holding in one hand, a cake that must weigh ten pounds, I swear; and, in the other hand, a recipe and a plastic bag filled w/ liquid dough, that so help me G-d, looked like a catheter bag.

What is all this about?

"Hi, this is a friendship cake." Judy oozed with cheerfulness.

"You take this dough, **knead it daily for ten days***, allowing the yeast to rise, and you make* **ten cakes** *and distribute them to people who you'd like to meet and make as a friend.."*

Well, folks, there is no one I want to befriend enough to knead dough for ten days and bake ten cakes.

"You're kidding, right?"

"I'm serious."

"Judy, is this like a chain cake letter?"

"Well, it is similar."

"You know, Judy, I'd like to be friends with you, but not at this cost. Why don't you take this cake back and that bag filled with that yechy dough liquid 'cause there is no way I want to participate in this mishigas (craziness). *I would gladly buy ten cakes to give away."*

"You're kidding?" Judy said with disbelief.

"No, I'm really not. I can't believe you found nine other people to accept this deal. Thank you anyway. We can still be friendly neighbors, but there is no way I am going to knead and bake ten cakes. Enjoy my share."

"No, you keep it, Phyllis. At least you're honest."

Well, folks, it takes all kinds; and to this day, Judy and I are good friends and neighbors, but when I see her coming with a cake and a recipe in her hand, I run the other way and will not open the door to her.

It's Flu Season Again

Is Typhoid Mary living amongst us in Florida?

Why did I stand in line for two hours with hundreds of people to get a flu shot in November?

The Flu is here…loud and clear.

If you don't have a cold, cough, fever, aches and pains, then you are one of the lucky ones. I'm sure your spouse is in bed *kvetching* or sleeping, or your neighbor, your canasta partner, your tennis or golf buddy is coughing away.

This virus is rampant. Some people are calling it a conspiracy. The northerners are bringing this germ down for vacation week. Our family and friends spend the week with us, and we all have a wonderful time. When they return to their homes up north, they leave us with a reminder of their visit. They leave us with the germ they were exposed to on their flight down here and we end up sick in bed for the following week.

Couldn't they have just brought us a gift? A bottle of wine? Flowers? Cocktail napkins with our name embossed?

We didn't need this gift. It's in every home in my community. I know because I can hear coughing and sniffling wherever I go. I hear it in the clubhouse, at the movies, on the tennis court, at the market. The flu doesn't want to leave. It lingers and lives with us for days and weeks.

My husband has been sick for eight days already. He's become part of the bedroom. I can only see his head sticking out of the covers (not such a terrible thing), but I can hear him coughing if I am standing outside my house, two miles away. I've left the "marriage bed." I don't want to sleep near him at night.

"If you need me, call me. I'm sleeping in the guest room. I don't want to get near you. I have to stay well to take care of you."

These are my parting words as I exit the bedroom for the fourteenth time this day.

I want to put him in a plastic bubble and quarantine our home for the benefit of others. I went to Walgreen's for more cough syrup. The shelf was almost empty of cold and sore throat remedies. Cough syrup was being rationed to customers.

I never made so much chicken soup in my life…not since the kids were younger and sick with sore throats and colds. Now, I'm doing it for my husband…and freezing some for me, if G-d forbid, I catch it.

And, what's happening up north? Now, they're coughing and sneezing. It caught up with them. Oy, yoy, yoy, I wish our northern friends would have brought us a bottle of wine instead.

Jewish.com

I began writing for the North Shore Jewish Journal in September, 2002, and since that date, I have become an encyclopedia of Jewish knowledge.

Prior to September I was your average Jewish lady from suburbia. Now I still remain your average Jewish lady from suburbia; however, I am also a *mayven* (expert) in all facets of Judaism. My limited knowledge of Jewish customs has expanded, and my Hebrew and Yiddish education has grown with every article I've written.

Would my parents be proud!! My kids could care less.

Writing my articles with a Jewish slant has been a true challenge for me although I grew up in a Jewish home, went to an orthodox *Shul* for holidays and attended Hebrew School for two years. As a grade school student, I *was* a crossing guard for William P. Connery School, but that didn't count for anything. There was nothing *Jewish* about that.

Help for writing for a Jewish newspaper came from surfing the web for Jewish sites. I was astounded at what I found via the internet. I was able to access a site for Jewish words that actually pronounces the Yiddish words for me through my speakers.

I found a Mitzvah Mall on the internet *where shopping is a mitzvah*. I have a friend who got so excited after hearing this because shopping is her life, and now she can rationalize her shopping sprees as performing mitzvahs.

I found out that s*chlemiel* and *shlemazel* are related. The *schlemie*l spills the soup on the *shlemazel*. *Shlmiel* means a fumbler and *slemazel* means an unlucky person. That makes sense. The *schlemiel* should not have been serving soup if he's a fumbler anyway.

I also learned that *halt din zoken* means hold your socks. Why did I need to know that? *A shaynem dank dir im pupik* means many thanks in your belly button. When would I ever use that expression? Talking to a pregnant woman? There must be a hidden meaning to this phrase.

In mitndrinen means right in the middle of everything. When I am speaking and someone interrupts me, I forget what I was saying. That is when I would use the term, *mitndrinen*. "*Mitndrinen,* she has to interrupt me so I lose my train of thought." How many senior moments do I need without help from someone who interrupts me?

Kvetch…that's a real good word. Even gentiles know the meaning of *kvetch.* A *kvetch* could be an ache or pain; and, then again, I know some *kvetches.* Some of them are really good friends.

When I enter a Jewish site via the internet, I am bombarded with *Hava Negilah.* I think that is the universal Yiddish song for Jewish sites. One site actually has a delivery service for kosher sushi with overnight FedEx service.

I enjoy hearing the Yiddish expressions spoken, albeit on my computer speakers. I remember my mother and father speaking them on occasion. They spoke in Yiddish so I wouldn't understand. Ludicrous, isn't it? I wish I had understood the Yiddish my parents spoke to one another. Now at my age, I'm trying to learn the expressions and pass them down to my grandchildren. Yiddish expressions are really delightful and many put a smile on your face.

Zay gezunt……*S*tay well, goodbye.

Cooking with Phyllis

Years ago I had the time and the patience to host a dinner party. Today it's a different story. First of all, the dining room table has to be extended. Years ago, that was *a piece of cake*. Who would think twice about opening up a dining room table?

Today, my husband and I have bad backs so we each sit at one end of the table, pull gently and tug at the ends until the table opens to the desired length. When we do this, we look at one another and say, *"Who would ever believe we would get to this stage?"* We laugh…half-heartedly.

Setting the table is a no-brainer.

Cooking is for a caterer, I've decided. My telephone never rings until I am knee-deep in preparing food and my hands are covered with *something*. How do I pick up the telephone with all the mish-mash on my hands? How do I *not* answer it? It could be an emergency.

I grab a paper towel and pick up the receiver. If I hesitate for a few extra seconds, the answering machine picks up, and I am competing with the message on the machine, *"Hello. Hello. Wait a minute. I'm here."*

It's usually a marketing survey call.

Do you know how time consuming making a salad is? Every piece of lettuce leaf should be washed (I know what to do; it doesn't mean I do it) and dried on a dish towel. Cucumbers have to be peeled without maiming oneself. Tomatoes washed; onions cut; olives drained; sprouts washed; peppers sliced. My kitchen looks like a tornado came through and left me everyone's garbage.

I also make chicken soup. I don't think I can give anyone the measurement of one item I put in my soup. My mother, *Olav Hashalom*, used to say, "A *shitarein (pinch)* of this; a *shitarein (pinch)* of that." That was her means of measuring. Her words meant, "*You have to watch me if you really want to know how much.*"

After the food is prepared, it must be covered with plastic wrap to be stored in the refrigerator. I take the beginning of the plastic roll and pull gently. Before I pull only six inches out of the box, it begins to curl in the middle and the sides of the plastic wrap are trying to meet. I cut it off on the serrated edge and pull another piece. I pull faster and harder trying to beat the sides of the plastic from meeting. I cut off a piece along with some of the skin of my finger and hold the wrap like a piece of paper hanging down so that the sides can not meet and mingle. Somehow I manage to cover the item and put it in the refrigerator which is about to burst from the amount of food.

"*Are we having an army for dinner?*" asks my husband.

"*It is better to have too much than not enough.*" (Heard that before, haven't you?)

After writing and reading this, I think we'll order in Chinese food.

The Infamous Junk Drawer

Variety is the spice of life. If we all lived and worked by the same rules, life would be boring.

We all worship differently. Some people attend reformed Temples, some go to Orthodox *Shuls,* and others worship at churches.

But some idiosyncrasies are common to every home; especially, a Jewish home.

How many of you have a ***junk drawer***? Among Jews, a lot of us have a drawer that has within it 400 yarmulkes from every affair we attended. Each one is a different color and each one says, *"From the Bar Mitzvah of Yankel So and So, 1982."*

How many of us have a collection of Passover Hagaddahs?

Each book is different in size and content. I still have the blue Maxwell House Hagaddahs. When you read from the the Hagaddah at the Sedar, everyone is reading from a different portion on a different page at the same time. No one knows where the leader is reading from in *his* Hagaddah since everyone has a different book.

How many of us have four or more menorahs…and an extra mezuzah hidden somewhere in one of our kitchen or dining room drawers?

Don't tell me you don't have magnets of every size and description on your refrigerator door? And, they keep falling off whenever you open and close the door. And, pictures of the children and grandchildren? They cover the surface of every table and wall in your home.

Let's return to the infamous *junk drawer*...

Within that drawer, I'll bet there are coupons galore; coupons for toilet paper, paper towels, aluminum foil, and some things we don't even need or use. I'll bet the majority of coupons have reached expiration date.

There are paper clips strewn all over the drawer, and dozens of pens and pencils that we can never find when we're on the telephone and need to use at a particular moment.

Slips of paper with phone numbers? We don't even remember to whom the phone numbers belong. Are they numbers to important doctors or restaurants? Who remembers? Are there scissors in that junk drawer? A piece of gum? A lifesaver? Two-cent stamps? Stamps with letters on them that we don't even remember the denomination of the stamp? Definitely, we have keys; at least two or three. We don't even know to what locks they belong.

G-d forbid, someone should touch something in that drawer.

"*That's my drawer. Get your own drawer.*"

No matter what religion you are, your home is no different from the home next door or to the home in the next town.

Do you know of one home where the male of the family replaces the empty roll of toilet paper...or refills the paper towel holder?

So you see, we're not all that different. No matter how and where we believe and pray, we all share the same *shtick!*

Where's that Sock?

Do you know what I find aggravating?

I find most disconcerting discovering a *Kleenex* was hiding in a pocket of my jeans after I washed my clothes in the washing machine. I checked the pockets!! How could this be?

Now all my clothes have pieces of wet tissue stuck to it.

Before I dry the clothes, should I check each piece of clothing for *Kleenex*? It's too difficult to remove when it's wet.

I transfer the wet laundry to the dryer, and after the proper drying time, I open the machine to find dry tissue stuck to every article of clothing in the dryer. The lint screen is covered with gray lint also. (Why is the lint always gray when the clothes are all different colors?) Removing the lint from the screen is easily accomplished by pulling it off in one piece. It's almost fun, if anything associated with household duties can be considered fun.

The clothing, however, has to be shaken outside so the tissue will fall off each sock and jersey. In the summer this is not such a terrible feat, but in the winter it is a different story. If I shake the clothes in the garage so that I don't have to brave the elements, the lint will get all over my cars and the garage floor. This is not a viable option. So, I must stand in the cold outside and shake each piece of clothing.

The icing on the cake: I am left holding ONE sock. Where is it? Is it stuck to a towel? I am not going to shake each one of them again. Is it in the dryer? I look in the dryer and call to it, *"Where are you, sock?"* At this point, I am walking a fine line between sanity and insanity.

No answer. What a surprise. Is it still in the washing machine? I peek in. No, it's not there. I check the dryer again. It's not there either. *Forget it already, Phyllis. It will turn up somewhere...probably stuck to a towel.* The sock probably cost two dollars, but it upset my routine.

Oh, my G-d, such tzorus (trouble*)*. I had better skip vacuuming before I suck up a chair.

Certain Tasks Only a Woman Can Perform

Do you know there are certain chores only a female is capable of performing? A male is unable to comprehend the complexities of certain tasks.

I lived in a home with a husband and two sons, one female to three males.

I am the only one in my house who knew how to change a roll of toilet paper. The men in my home did not know how to remove the empty roller and locate the place where the rolls of toilet paper are kept. They believed the toilet paper was kept in a secret place.

A man can fix a plugged-up toilet but the menial task of changing a roll of toilet paper is beyond him. I could leave a roll of toilet paper as close as possible to the roller. It didn't matter. It could have been sitting on top of the old roll. I'm still the one who replaced it.

Do you live in a house with stairs leading to the bedroom? Do you leave items on the stairs to bring up at a later time in the day? Does anyone, other than you, ever bring up those things without being asked or told? A man could fall over them walking up the stairs but still would not think of bringing them upstairs with him. A woman is the only one who knows how to carry those items up the stairs. They aren't heavy; it's usually clothes; but a man is physically unable to lift them from the stair.

Has anyone in your home ever started the laundry other than you, put the laundry into the dryer *without being told or asked to?*

No. You, the woman, are the only one who knows how to do laundry. It's a "classified" process.

How about running the dishwasher? That's a hard chore. Detergent has to be located and put in a secret spot in the lid of the dishwasher. Only a woman knows how to achieve that momentous undertaking. You are the brains behind running a dishwasher, although it only requires a dash of detergent, the closing of the dishwasher door, and pushing the "start" button. Why is it so difficult?

Change the linen on a bed? Does a man even know where the linen closet is?

"Go down the hall, take a left, turn the handle on the door, open the door, and remove the linens."

"Which ones?" asks Man.

"The top ones."

"How many?"

"Forty six... **Two.** *How many do you think? You sleep on them every single night of the year. 365 days times your age, you've been sleeping on linens. Dear G-d.!!!"*

No answer from Man.

I take the initiative. *"Forget it."*

It's easier for a woman to do this simple task. It takes twice as long when a man helps. Is that why the woman is the one who changes the toilet rolls?

In the days of the cavemen, Man hunted for the meal while Woman cooked at the fire that Man made for Woman before he left the cave to hunt.

Today Man sits at the computer or T.V. while Woman *shleps* to the market and then cooks the meal at the fire that Woman turns the dial to ignite.

It's really not so terrible.

Besides, at this stage in my life, what woman cooks? Women, my age, have learned to make reservations or buy *already-cooked, just warm- in- the- oven* food.

And, I'm still the only one who changes the toilet paper.

I Remember When...

When I was younger, **many years** younger, I lived in the city of Lynn, Massachusetts. I remember going to a Saturday matinee every weekend. My mother would give me a dollar, and I would walk to downtown Lynn with my girlfriends and spend the entire afternoon at the movie theatre. With one dollar, I would gain admission to the theatre, buy popcorn and chocolate candy bars, and still have small change left for the bus ride home. The bus would not take me the entire way home for a dime so I walked from the end of the bus line to my home. It was only nine blocks of skipping on the sidewalk with my friends.

I remember standing in line to get into the theatre, talking to all the other kids who were also waiting in line. We all knew one another from public school, and we loved to talk and *fool around* while waiting to gain entrance. When the theatre doors opened and our money collected by the ticket seller, we would run inside and choose our seats.

We would sit through two black and white movies and be *in heaven* for the afternoon. We would watch cowboy and Indian flicks such as *Tom Mix* and *The Lone Ranger, Movietone* newsreels, *The Three Stooges, The Little Rascals*, and scary movies. We would eat our candy and throw our wrappers at the kids sitting in front of us, boo the villains, cheer the heroes, and the time would fly.

Imagine sitting through two movies now. I can hardly sit through *one* movie now without my back aching or my bladder bursting. I still eat popcorn, but now it gets caught under my "bridge," and I have to leave the movie in the best part to floss my teeth in the ladies room.

As for the younger generation, no longer are there downtown theatres that parents would allow their youngsters to attend. The kids are driven to multiplex theatres in the suburbs. They are told not to talk to anyone, to stay together, to wait outside the theatre until they are picked up by the assigned parent who will *drive* them home.

Walk home? This younger generation doesn't know how to walk anywhere. Nothing recreational is within walking distance; and, besides, there are no local buses to take them anywhere.

How times have changed...

I'll bet you remember those Saturday matinees too...makes you smile, doesn't it? They're nice memories.

Have You Ever Been to a "Jewish Pot Luck Dinner?"

Let me tell you, the food was better than any restaurant I've been to in Boston or in Florida.

Every woman received an assignment to make a course for the entire group.

So, *nu*, are you going to make something *not wonderful* if your friends are going to silently judge what gastronomic specialty you have concocted for the evening?

Of course not.

Each woman spent hours deciding what to make after being given her assigned course. She *shlepped* only to the finest of stores to buy the proper ingredients; and, after hours upon hours of preparing it, she completed her *creme de la creme* with a magnificent presentation of her course.

Boy, was that a meal. Each course looked like a photo from *Bon Appetit* or any gourmet magazine. Every morsel of food tasted as if the finest chefs from Paris were brought in for the evening to prepare the delicacies.

Now there are some women who work and have no time to cook, and there are some women who just don't like to cook, but these women know where to *shop*. So these women bought their assignment. *Oy,* were those foods wonderful too. They went only to the best of caterers for their dishes.

Fine wine was flowing; conversation was easy, compliments were being exchanged, and "*Oh, it was nothing*" was repeatedly spoken from the mouths of the ladies. The conversation was comfortable and typical when six close couples get together for an evening.

The women discussed menopause and soy products, and the men discussed business, politics, and retirement. Now all of us are in our fifties and sixties, and of course, we don't look it. We exercise faithfully to look young and vital. However, out of six couples present that evening, three of us took turns having hot flashes. We looked like fan dancers with rosiola. We would have loved a cold shower.

This was our first Jewish Pot Luck dinner, and truthfully, the evening was a success. It was a success not only because the food was wonderful, but the fact that six couples enjoyed one another's company. That was *what made the evening*.

I highly recommend it...

This is a Security Guard?

I was accosted last night by a security guard in the parking lot of *Publix Super Market*.

The guard was younger than my sons, better looking than Brad Pitt, and built like Arnold Schwartzenegger. He was wearing a white t-shirt with muscles bulging and black shorts with other muscles bulging (use your imagination).

However, he was driving a golf cart with an awning, which kind of dimmed my erotic thoughts; although, the car did have bright yellow lights on the top.

I was sitting in the car around 9:00 p.m., parked parallel to the sidewalk waiting for Jerry, who ran into the market for a lottery ticket. The lot was almost empty, and I said I'd wait outside near the door. Another car, an SUV, was parked in front of me. All of a sudden, I see bright yellow lights in my rear-view mirror, and this "kid" is motioning for me to move my car.

Was he kidding? There were hardly any cars in the entire lot. The "kid" looked like he was going to have a stroke with his hands waving up and down. This, I didn't need. I moved the car. He approached the car in front of me. Well, this driver was not going to move. The young man, the security guard, dressed in shorts, was just about ready to smash his little cart into the SUV when finally the SUV moved.

Thank G-d, the guard wasn't allowed to carry a gun or he would have shot the driver for parking there for three minutes.

I was reminded of the police at Boston's Logan Airport who make you move your car when there are no other cars around. They have to demonstrate their authority. They are our men in uniform, but it's a shame that the uniform does not make the man.

This muscle-bound "kid" in his golf cart probably had the IQ of a high school student and the disposition and temper of a child. I got his name and submitted it to the Massachusetts State Police for employment at Logan Airport. When I arrive at Logan, with my luck, I'll probably see him there. He'll make me move my car again.

There is a postscript to this incident.

Today I was back at the *Publix* market. I feel like I live there. Anyway, whom do you think drove by in his little golf cart? Right, **The Terminator** in those gorgeous pair of tight black shorts and his t-shirt.

I figured he'd find something wrong with the way I was driving today too. Instead, he smiled at me when he drove by. He was drinking a milk shake or some concoction in a plastic cup through a straw.

This is the hunk who frightened me. He blew the image today. Anyone who drinks a milk shake through a straw is not going to frighten me anymore. He is a *wuss* who happens to work in an authoritative position. I'm applying tomorrow for the same position as he. I can drive a golf cart and I sure as heck can scare drivers with my *moyel* (mouth).

I'm going to fill out an application as soon as I finish working on developing my biceps.

"*Move your car, mister. The BocaYente is in charge.*"

E-mailing Has Become a Way of Life for Some People

I am one of those people. I communicate with friends and relatives more often by e-mail than by telephone. I don't use this avenue of telecommunications because of the cost. I use it for convenience.

For instance, how many times have you called someone and their telephone line is constantly busy? They're usually talking to someone or using their computer.

The *e-mail line* is never busy. I don't have to keep calling and calling until the person at the other end answers the phone.

By the time someone finally answers at the other end of a telephone, thirty or forty minutes later, I have forgotten what I wanted to say.

I am never put on *hold* for *call-waiting*. What an insult to my ego.

"Phyllis, hold on for a minute. I have another call coming in."

You mean it's more important than my telephone call? There have been times the other party never came back to my call. I took the hint. I hung up. Usually, I received an apology call thirty minutes later from the person to whom I was speaking.

"It was my daughter calling from up north. I had to talk."

Couldn't she have called her daughter back after she finished our conversation?

How about long distance calls via cell phone?

We've all signed up for thousands of minutes on our *Sprint* or *Cingular* service. We have to make the minutes count so we use our cell phone to call our friends who live out of state. We look for people throughout the country to call.

"*Why waste the minutes?*" we ask ourselves. We forget it's only five cents a minute, or even less, to use our house phone and have clear transmission. At times, we can hardly understand one full sentence when we speak via cell phone.

The conversation usually goes like this.

"Hi, Phyllis, ……going on? Have you…….from the ……lately? Is the ……… still……..? Are you ……… to………next………"

"Nancy, you're breaking up !! I can't hear you. Send me an e-mail."

I find each one of us treats e-mailing in different ways. One friend thinks I remember exactly what I e-mailed to her two days ago.

Her responses read like this:

"Hi, Phyllis…..

She said O.K.

Loved that joke.

The story is only a rumor….

I sent the package to her.

Have a good day….."

What is she talking about? Who said O.K? O.K to what? What joke? What story? What package? To whom? *Argh!*

Thank goodness her e-mail address is at the top of the e-mail or I would have no idea who even sent the e-mail.

I love the *Fwd* e-mails. Some come with 20 >>>>>>. I stopped opening those e-mails months ago. It would take two minutes for a person to clean up the original e-mail and forward it, but it's easier to just hit forward rather than copy, delete, and paste. When I do spend the time opening the *fwd* e-mail, it's usually an e-mail I received from another individual two weeks ago.

I guess the other fault I have with e-mail is the time it takes to send or receive a photo or graphic via telephone line. I send and receive my transmissions via cable but there are times I could take a nap while the computer is sending. It is so slow. I could wash a floor (G-d forbid) or vacuum my house waiting for each transmission to finish. But there is no other way for me to show photos of my grandchildren to my friends and family who live in New England.

Send it by snail mail…no way !!!!!

Well, now that you've had to wait for this transmission with my graphic at the top, did you wash your floor?

G-d forbid !!

Serious Ramblings of the Boca Yente

The Totem Pole of Priorities

I lost my cleaning lady.

I didn't lose her walking on the street. What I mean to say is she left me. She moved back to Colombia.

When I told some friends what had happened, they asked what I was going to do. This was terrible news to them. They were more distraught than I felt. I looked at them with disbelief and thought, *"What are their priorities in life?"* I really wasn't worried. Have I finally become wiser with age? Have I finally learned what's important and what's not important in the hierarchy of life?

No one is indispensable...especially when they *think* they're indispensable.

Sixteen years ago, my husband, Jerry, was upset because his secretary who worked for him for twelve years was leaving due to illness. He was upset because she was sick, but he was also upset because he had an office to run, and he didn't think she could ever be replaced.

He asked me to fill in until he found a replacement. I left twenty-five years later. I watched over that office like a hawk since it was our "bread and butter," and he never had to worry again. I hired office staff when it was needed and I took over chores he despised. I left him to his cutting and triming. (Remember, he is a periodontist.) The office problem was solved.

The loss of a cleaning lady is not a matter of life and death. The loss of an employee is not a critical matter. A broken leg is not a permanent health problem. (Ask me. Jerry's broken his leg three times). An appointment cancelled, when you've planned your whole day around it is upsetting, granted. However, these situations and many more like them are not major crises. Yet some people treat them as such. They are inconveniences in our daily routine, but they are not life-threatening and worth the aggravation and emotional feelings we feed into them.

We should sit down and evaluate our totem pole of priorities. I think many of us would be surprised to realize the wasted energy we put into trivial problems. I did a self-evaluation some months ago because of some minor health concerns, and I realized I have to weigh what is and what isn't important in life. It's not an easy task...especially for a Type A controlling personality. I have also learned that I must try to forgive certain people for their shortcomings. I know darn well I do not have it in me to forget; especially, if I was wounded. What is sad, *we usually don't realize our priorities are askew until something "terrible" does happen to us...and then we wake up and smell the roses.*

I was proud of myself when I thought, "*O.K., I'll just have to find another cleaning lady.*" No big deal.

By the way, I found one within 24 hours. Her name? NO WAY !!

A Lovely Place to Be

I entered through the sliding glass doors of the Jewish Rehabilitation Center and walked down the lengthy corridor.

I stood far enough back so that I could see her but she did not see me. She was sitting in her favorite chair, a comfortably stuffed green leather chair. She chose that one for its location in the room. Sitting there, she could see all the activity going on around her. She was wearing her walking sneakers that I bought for her. Of course, now one sneaker had a slit cut on the outer side so that her bunion could sneak through and not cause her pain when she walked. Her white socks were folded at the ankle, very neatly as always.

I remember the day I brought her the sneakers.

"Sneakers? I don't wear sneakers. You know that. I have my pumps or my leather Rockports that I like to wear."

I had to convince her that sneakers would be more appropriate and it would be acceptable for me to cut a slit in them for her comfort. She was afraid people would talk if they saw her with a ripped shoe.

She was wearing her pastel blue pants with the elastic waist and her matching sweatshirt with the dogs embroidered on the front. I could see her shirt was stained with food although she was unaware of it. She would have been so embarrassed if she knew she was sitting in clothes that were soiled.

She always noticed my appearance, if *I* were dressed properly or if *I* had make-up on, no matter what time of day.

Her hands were folded together but her fingers were moving back and forth looking for her wedding ring, the ring she had worn for the past 62 years. It was not there on her finger, but maybe she could still feel the imprint where it had always been. For fear of being stolen, it was resting in my jewelry box at my home. She had on her faux pearl earrings that she wore daily.

It seemed to me as I was observing her that she was not fully aware of her surroundings. She was looking straight ahead staring into space, focused somewhere in the past. Her lips were turned up just a bit at the ends, and you knew she was somewhere happy in her thoughts. She had no lipstick on which was unusual for her, and she was sitting with the newspaper spread open in her lap.

The pages were probably open to the society page or the theatre section. I couldn't see from where I was standing and observing her, but I was happy to see she was making an attempt to read the news. She fidgeted a bit, looked around at the others in the room, almost as if she knew she were being watched, arched her back slightly to make herself more comfortable in the big club chair, and sat back. Her facial expression never changed.

She fingered the Jewish star and engraved gold pendant on the chain around her neck. Her children, at her 50th anniversary party, gave the star and necklace to her as a present. That event was twelve years ago.

I could remember that party at the *Kernwood Country Club* with the band playing, the champagne overflowing, and the tables decorated with beautiful centerpieces. She was lovely in her dress; and her husband, at her side, was dressed smartly in a dark suit and tie. Everyone surrounding them was smiling and laughing. She was probably entertaining them with one of her humorous stories or one-liners at which she was so adept.

I realized I was standing and watching this lovely older woman with the same expression on my face as she had on her face. Maybe these moments are an escape from the present or a walk in the past, but it was lovely place to be.

I had been totally oblivious of my surroundings for the past few minutes.

Time to return to the present...

I entered the room at the Jewish Rehabilitation Center, a nursing home, and I walked toward her. She noticed me approaching, and the glaze over her eyes seemed to melt away. She looked around briefly as if to get a handle on *where she was* and she watched me come closer to her. Her smile intensified, her eyes shined with recognition, and her hands unfolded with palms open and extended.

I looked down as I bent to kiss her hello.

"*Hi, Ma.*"

"*Oh, hi, Phyllis, I was just thinking of you.*"

"*So was I, Ma. I was thinking of you too.*" I paused and looked down at her.

I blurted out, "*Do you want to go to lunch, just you and me?*"

"*I'd love that, Phyllis.*"

"*Me too, Ma.*"

My mother died three days later. I was at her side holding her hand.

The Air is Heavy in a Waiting Room

I clenched my hands into two tight fists, raised them above my head and in a throaty whisper, exclaimed, *"Yes!"*

I was Rocky after winning the boxing match in ten rounds. I was walking on a cushion of clouds, no floor beneath my feet, only buoyant air.

My yearly mammogram was negative.

I was dressed in a pair of slacks, socks and loafers, and wearing only a thin blue and white bathrobe covering my naked torso. I had just left a dimly-lit cubicle with three x-ray view boxes attached to a wall in front of a radiologist sitting at a desk. He looked like he was recently bar-mitzvahed. Either I was getting older or the doctors were graduating younger. The radiologist reviewed my radiogram and told me the results were good.

"Everything looks clean."

Those are magical words to a woman. They are more meaningful than any gift of diamonds and gold. Those words lighten your steps, take the weight off your shoulders, give you hope for tomorrow and thanks for today.

My yearly check-up is performed at the *Sagoff Breast Clinic* in Jamaica Plains, MA. You enter a large brick building, climb one flight of stairs, and enter a narrow room with three receptionists sitting behind desks. You fill out the usual forms, have a seat and await the calling of your name.

No woman makes eye contact with another woman, unless they sneak a look. Women are sitting with open paperback novels. They appear to be reading but trust me, they are not concentrating on the written words.

Your name is called.

You enter the inner sanctum, go into a dressing room and try to figure out how to don a dressing gown with three armholes. The last time you looked, you had only two arms. You follow the directions printed on a piece of paper taped to the wall and manage to get into this strange garment made for aliens from outer space. You put on a thin bathrobe made for people 250 lbs or better. The robe is hanging to the floor, the sleeves are down to your knees, and you belt it with the narrowest string you've ever seen.

You proceed to the inner waiting room with eight or ten other women who are dressed just like you. Truthfully, no one cares how she looks at this time. No one actually looks or sees one another since each woman is locked into her own secret hopes and thoughts.

At my visit last year, I was called back into the room for a re-take. My head started to spin with horrendous thoughts, and my legs turned to jelly. The technician reassured me that it was just a minor spot the doctor wanted to check. *Nothing related to an abnormality in the breast is minor*, I thought.

This, thank G-d, was minor. It turned out to be a calcification deposit. I lost two lbs. just waiting for the results of this *minor* abnormality.

While waiting for the results, I looked around the waiting room. My heart was pounding in my chest. I thought to myself that, given the statistics, someone in this room was going to receive a bad report. The percentages are there. I didn't want it to be me. Was I wishing it upon some other woman in this room? I wouldn't wish it upon my worst enemy, but I still didn't want it to be me.

The air is heavy in a waiting room. No one really talks to one another. The body language of the women is: *"Don't talk to me now, please. I'm tied up in my thoughts. No inane conversation. I just want a good report and to get the hell out of here."*

A man can sympathize. A woman can empathize.

One light moment did occur.

One of the women was called into the doctor's office, and when she came out, she had a grin from ear to ear. Everyone woman sitting there knew she had received a good report.

She took a left turn rather than a right turn and walked out through the doors to the *outer* waiting room by mistake. *Remember, she was dressed in that blue and white striped bathrobe with nothing on from the waist up.* Two seconds later, she came flying back into the inner room.

She looked at all of us and said with a smile on her face, *"I gave them a show. Who cares?"*

She was right. She wasn't embarrassed. She was on a high. She got a "Clean Bill of Health."

So did I, thank G-d…

Now I just have to wait another 365 days for the next mammogram.

Listen to Us Once in a While

We went with another couple to dinner at a local restaurant. The tables are very close to one another. A father and his college-age son were seated at the next table. It felt like we were seated at a table for six.

I did not mean to eavesdrop, nor did anyone at my table, but the conversation between the father and son could be heard by all of us.

Evidently, the father who lives in Maryland was visiting his son who attends Tufts University in Boston. Bits and pieces of their conversation were so typical that all four of us could say, *"Been there, done that."*

The father, at one point in the conversation said, *"I can look myself in the mirror and like what I see. How can you? Can you live with yourself? You have one set of grandparents. Is it so much to ask of you to spend the holidays with them? They live so near you now."*

"Dad, I don't tell you what to do and who to spend Rosh Hashanah with. I'm old enough to make my own decisions."

"They won't live forever. Don't you have feelings?"

"If you continue, Dad, I'm walking out of the restaurant."

Now there is silence for a few minutes, and the four of us begin talking. We forgot we came with one another. We were busy eating and listening. We had become totally involved in the life and lifestyle of the father and son sitting beside us.

The father continued his plea.

"*The school empties out at the holidays anyway.*"

The four of us stopped talking and began listening again. We felt like voyeurs but we felt like we were part of his family. We knew our behavior was not commendable, and we tried not to listen but we wanted this father to win his case.

The father was so right. The young man's grandparents would not live forever. It would give them so much *nachas* to have their grandson with them at *Yontif*. Was it so much to ask of the young man?

The father and son had such a serious discussion that the four of us didn't know what we were eating, and we didn't even enjoy the dinner.

We didn't enjoy it because the son walked out.

The father paid the bill and left the restaurant.

The father lost the argument. We knew the son was not going to his grandparents' home for the Jewish holidays.

We don't even know this boy and his father, nor do we know his grandparents, and we probably will never see them again. However, we could sympathize and empathize with the father. He wanted to make his son's grandparents happy. He knew that the greatest joy for a grandparent is to spend some time with their grandchild. It's special. It's a personal bond that is always remembered by the grandchild and the grandparent.

I can still remember my *bobbie* playing card games with me. If only grandchildren could understand what it means to be a grandparent, but they don't learn until they are grandparents…sometimes, too late.

Too late for this young man! He ruined our dinner…and our evening!

I Can Travel... Alone

I recently had an interesting visit. I traveled up north...alone.

My husband injured his back, for a change, and he was unable to sit on an airplane for any length of time. We were scheduled to fly to Marblehead, north of Boston, for my sister's grandson's Bar Mitzvah. We were going to stay with my sister and her husband who also live in Marblehead, where we lived for the past 31 years.

How could I not go to this mitzvah? It was *my* family. So I went alone.

I left on a Wednesday and stayed until Sunday morning. I experienced some unusual feelings being back in my hometown.

One evening I spent with my girlfriends at dinner sans husbands and we *yented* away about everyone and anyone. Oh, you would have too...admit it. That was a 'fun" night.

Another day I drove to my son's house and spent almost the entire day playing with my three-year-old granddaughter and enjoying the laughter of my three-month-old grandson. I was greeted with little *hentees* (hands) encircling my neck, *"Grandma, I love you. I love you. I missed you. Did you bring any puzzles or toys? Can we play school in my room?"*

Do you know a grandmother who would have come empty-handed? I *shlepped* toys on the plane by the bagful. The grateful arms of my granddaughter around my neck were worth the 1600 miles I trekked via airplane, especially since my flight was delayed three hours due to a *meshugina* snow storm in Boston in the middle of April.

I stayed overnight at the home of my sister and brother-in-law, and we talked to one another...really talked, not just superficial conversation. Trite as it may seem, we bonded!! My sister and I always loved one another, may not have agreed with one another all the time, yet we were always there for one another in crises and difficult family situations. I think we both understood one another after these past few days better than we ever had in all the years gone by.

Being at the Bar Mitzvah was the most emotional experience of the weekend.

It was held at the temple where our boys had their Bar Mitzvah, and where one of our sons got married. My husband and I had been members for over 31 years. I felt as if I had come *home*.

It was the same Rabbi and Cantor officiating who led our congregation before our moving to Florida which is unusual. The clergy usually last just so many years before offending some one of the power brokers (big *machers*) in a congregation...and then, off they go to a different congregation!!

I recognized all the melodies which is unusual since every temple has its *own tune* of the *same* prayer...the same prayer that has been sung for centuries. I think *Adon Olom* has over 100 different tunes throughout each and every state except North Dakota, where there are no Jewish people (just joking).

The temple seat felt good under my *tuchas*. It was familiar. The faces of the congregants were all friendly, warm and welcoming. I was surrounded by my sons, one sitting on each side of me; and, my sister and her clan were all present and sitting near me. The Bar Mitzvah boy was wonderful, by the way.

I had an *aliyah* during the service, and as I stood beside the open ark on the *bima* (pulpit) and looked at the congregation, I knew I had returned ***home***.

I boarded the aircraft the next morning. I was ready to return to my husband and sunny Florida and all the new friends I made, and I was happy I had gone back for a piece of my memories.

Time to Visit the Folks

The *dog days* of August are coming to a close, and it's time to start thinking about returning to Florida. I don't think we will remain in Marblehead for the holidays; we will attend a temple down south. I'll miss sitting with my family in temple and sharing dinner with them after New Year services. I hope they understand that my heart is with them, my family; but my home is now in Florida.

Guess I will go visit the folks and say good-bye today. I'll take along a *yarmulkah* (head covering) and a *sidur* (Hebrew book) so I can chant the proper prayers. I like to go when it's quiet there (although I doubt it's ever noisy), and no one else is around.

I talk to my folks, tell them what's happening, ask their advice on certain family issues. I don't have to worry that an argument will ensue if they disagree. They don't talk back, although I know what their words would be if they could answer me.

I'll tell them all about their grandchildren and their great grandchildren. They never had the chance to meet the great grandchildren but they know all about them since I am forever talking about the *einicles*.

When I return to Florida, I still talk to my folks. I talk to them when I'm driving the car. Crazy place, right? But it's quiet, and I like to have my private time with them.

Sometimes, my eyes mist over, and I have a hard time seeing the cars in front of me. That's when I know I've been spending too much time on conversation and not enough time concentrating on the road.

Well, I'm almost at my folks' place now. I see the gates are open, as usual. It's quiet today since it's still early for family members to visit other family members. There's still a few more weeks before the Jewish holidays.

I'm sure you figured out where I am today.

I'm at the cemetery. I've come to see my folks before I leave for Florida. I know my sister will visit them while I'm gone, but I will not be able to visit them until next summer. But I'll be talking to them. They're in my heart, and I take them everywhere. They even come to Florida with me and enjoy the sunshine.

Home is Where the Mezuzah is

It's nice to be back on the North Shore.

I see familiar faces, familiar street signs, the same walkers, runners, and joggers as last year. The people are just a little older...as I am.

My husband and I are renting in the same condo in downtown Marblehead as last year; and as I sit at my computer, I am looking at the same photos. It's strange to look at pictures on the wall of unknown family members. There are wedding pictures (I don't know the couple); there are baby pictures (I don't recognize this baby); there are group pictures in foreign places (who are they? where was it taken?) This year the photos are beginning to look familiar. I feel like I belong to this family.

When we returned this season, I realized what was most heart-warming was the mezuzah on the door.

I feel the mezuzah is such a welcome and warm symbol, and I never really knew the *full* meaning behind it until I found information on the internet that it is a *mitzvah* to place a mezuzah on the doorpost of a house.

I learned that the words of the *Shema* (*Hear, O Israel*) are the words written on a tiny scroll of parchment within the mezuzah. The scroll is then rolled up, placed in the case, so that the letter *Shin* is visible and is also written on the outside of the case. The scroll must be handwritten in a special style of writing and must be placed in the case to *fulfill* the mitzvah. The case and scroll are then nailed or affixed to the right side doorpost on an angle.

Why is the mezuzah affixed at an angle? The rabbis could not decide whether it should be placed horizontally or vertically, so they compromised! It figures.

Every time you pass through a doorway with a mezuzah on it, you should touch the mezuzah and then kiss the fingers that touched it, expressing love and respect for G-d and his *mitzvot* and reminding yourself of the *mitzvot* contained within them.

I guess, to a Jew like myself, seeing a mezuzah on the doorpost of a home where I will be living for three months, sparks a feeling of warmth and welcome.

Now I really feel like I'm part of their family photographs. I may even hang a photo of *our* own family and see if, when they return, they detect an addition to their clan. I don't even mind watering their 300 plants for them either. *We're family.*

It's nice to return to the north shore, if only for the summer. I may reside in Florida nine months of the year, but *Home is Where the Heart Is*...and my heart is here.

My Favorite Story
Originally written 1978

"Let Me Tell You About My Affair"

I always wanted to have an affair. I wasn't even fussy with whom, but for my generation, it was considered forbidden fruit. Today it's not even a delicacy.

So I had an affair. I made my sons' Bar Mitzvahs.

What, you thought I was going to write about something else?

I reserved the date of the Bar Mitzvah with the Temple the night I conceived. Barring earthquakes, tornados, or any natural disasters, the date I chose is the date I had to have the affair… thirteen years later. Yes, it is carved in stone.

Once the date is selected, a caterer has to be chosen. There were just so many *in* caterers at the time, and I interviewed each one to make sure I made the right decision. I *shlepped* my mother who drove me crazy because nothing I ever chose was right with her. I could have taken my husband but he could have cared less about a menu. Actually, the food was the easiest part. I asked the caterer what he would suggest, and I chose everything he recommended.

The music was the most difficult task. My son wanted a DJ. I wanted a band, and my husband wanted me to stop arguing with my son and with my mother, not necessarily in that order.

I became the music *mayven* (expert) of the North Shore. I went to every party and listened to every band and DJ that came "down the pike." We made our selection and drew up a contract insisting that, barring the band leader's death, he would show up in person. No ifs, ands, or buts.

What to wear was the next decision in planning my affair. All of a sudden, my son's Bar Mitzvah became...*My Affair.*

I went from store to store; shopped all over New England until I found the perfect dress. It was a known fact that if I didn't find a magnificent dress, there would be no Bar Mitzvah. I finally found the dress, and after driving twenty times back and forth for fittings, the dress was perfect.

Suits for the males is a *piece of cake,* right? Wrong. My son, who only lived in jeans, wanted a suit with European styling. He always hated shopping, and now he is standing and modeling suits in front of every available mirror in the clothing store. I thought someone had snatched my real son, when I wasn't looking, and left me this Prince.

My husband? He didn't want a suit. Why couldn't he wear one that he had in the closet? I dragged him to Boston, to a lovely men's store, had him try on a suit, and all of a sudden, I was watching the Prince's father turn into the King. What was happening to these male egos? He was becoming G-d's gift to women. He was turning this way and that way preening in front of the mirror.

The Guest List: Oh, this is the worst part. Where do you draw the line? Do you need your husband's family? Do you need your neighbors? And, now another opinion enters the ring, a voice to be reckoned with: My Mother, the grandmother of the Bar Mitzvah boy.

She is no pushover either. She has drawn the line at fourth cousins and her friends from the beauty parlor. She insists on relatives I don't even know but she says she can never look them in the face if I don't invite them.

My mother-in-law was easier. She told me to invite whomever I wanted from her family. She didn't care. She didn't know half of them anyway.

Then there were the invitations. I wanted them to be classy and *smart*. I ran from post office to post office to choose stamps that would be color-coordinated with the envelopes and with the calligraphy. The stamps had to be appropriate for a Bar Mitzvah. Don't ask me what makes them appropriate. I just knew the invitation couldn't bear the stamp with two swans intertwined.

I handled the invitations with rubber gloves, I swear. I kept the invitations in a large, clean box, carefully protecting them with tissue paper. I brought them directly to the post office, eliminating the mail box, and what happened next was a shock to my system.

The postman picked up the invitations with his ink-stained hands, bound them with the smallest elastic I had ever seen and threw them in a large container with other mail. Color drained from my face, I became light-headed, and tears were welling in my eyes. I knew at that time I was walking a fine line between sanity and insanity.

Seating Plan: A nightmare !! No one wanted to sit with anyone in his or her own family. She doesn't talk to this one. He doesn't talk to that one. I didn't want to talk to anyone by this time! And, where do you sit the clergy? You sit them with the fourth cousins who are relatively intelligent, void of humor, eat with their utensils, and do not utter obscenities.

The Day of the Twilight Bar Mitzvah

It is 8:00 a.m. and the first thing on the agenda is a run to the hairdresser for a final "do" and a manicure. Everyone at the salon wishes me well on my affair.

I was a wreck. Will the food be hot? Will the photographer be in the way? Will the band leader really show up? Will the flowers be too tall for the table and interfere with dinner conversation? Will the weather be nice? It shouldn't rain, please.

And, my son, the Bar Mitzvah boy, where is he?

He's in the bathroom sick to his stomach. He entered that sanctuary at 5:30 a.m., and it's now 11:00 a.m. He left once to eat breakfast, which was a waste of food, and he left again to go to the "stylist" for a haircut. Twenty times he asked me why he has to go through with the Bar Mitzvah. Twenty times I gave him the same answer, *"Your father already paid the caterer, the band leader and the florist. We have our clothes. Your grandmother invited all of the North Shore; and you know your Haftorah. You will be fine."*

The sun is shining. I keep looking out at the weather as if I were on civil defense duty at the local bomb shelter. I am afraid to answer the telephone in case someone is calling to tell me they can't come...after I ordered their meal.

It is now 2:00 p.m. My son's mental condition is deteriorating. His face is a ghastly white.

It is time for me to get dressed. Today I will wear make-up, tons of it. Now I am not a make-up person, but today I am going to use every cosmetic in my bathroom drawer...eye liner, eye shadow, rouge, the whole shmear. I go the gamut, and I look in the mirror.

Oy, I look terrific; of course, I don't have my glasses on yet. I must get into the dress without getting make-up on it, and I accomplish that feat like a contortionist. I put on my twenty rings, three diamond necklaces, forty bracelets, and I'm gorgeous. I'm also weighted down with so much jewelry that my back is going into spasm.

The men come out of their respective bedrooms "dressed to the nines" in their suits, and *tarke*, they look good!

We enter the car gingerly so as not to brush up against the side of the car and soil our outfits.

"*G-d forbid, you should have had the car washed*," are the loving words I whisper to my husband.

We arrive at the temple, and we all begin to take deep breaths to ward off fainting and nausea...except my husband who is laissez-faire about the whole event. Later he will be nauseous when he signs the checks. Guests arrive and they try to decide on which side to sit. What is the difference? It's not a wedding. It's a Bar Mitzvah.

The ceremony is beginning, and my son has left his private sanctuary for the temple sanctuary. His color is off-white. Those family members with speaking aliyahs are beginning to look like my son...off-white. This is turning into a beige Bar Mitzvah.

My son is called to the pulpit. My husband and I are on each side of him. I can hear everyone's heartbeat. My son recites his *haftorah* with magnificence. I look out at the 2000 guests. My mother is crying. My aunt is still looking for a seat, and my canasta club is talking and checking out everyone's clothes.

I want to yell at the congregation and say, "*Look, I did it. I went the thirteen rounds with my son...and we both lasted. Please, dear G-d, let me last another 130 rounds...and let me plan his son's Bar Mitzvah. After all, I am now a Bar Mitzvah Mayven.*"

I finally had My Affair.